The Properties of *Othello*

The
Properties
of *Othello*

James L. Calderwood

The University of Massachusetts Press

Amherst

Copyright © 1989 by
The University of Massachusetts Press
All rights reserved
Printed in the United States of America
LC 88-27767
ISBN 0-87023-666-0
Designed by Edith Kearney
Set in Linotron Plantin by Keystone Typesetting, Inc.
Printed by Thomson-Shore, Inc.
and bound by John H. Dekker & Sons, Inc.

Library of Congress Cataloging-in-Publication Data
Calderwood, James L.
    The properties of Othello.
    Bibliography: p.
    Includes index.
    1. Shakespeare, William, 1564–1616. Othello.
2. Property in literature. 3. Self in literature.
I. Shakespeare, William, 1564–1616. Othello. II. Title
PR2829.C29   1989   822.3'3   88–27767
ISBN 0–87023–666–0

British Library Cataloguing in Publication data is available.

To Norman Rabkin

Contents

Acknowledgments

I'm grateful to the University of California, Irvine, for a sabbatical leave during which I wrote most of this book. I'm also grateful to Graham Bradshaw for suggesting I write it in the first place and for many helpful suggestions afterwards. Barbara A. Mowat of the *Shakespeare Quarterly*, T. H. Adamowski of the *University of Toronto Quarterly*, and the editors of *Shakespeare Studies* (Japan) have kindly allowed me to reprint material that appeared earlier and somewhat differently in their journals: "Speech and Self in *Othello*," *SQ* 38, 3 (Autumn 1987); "Appalling Property in *Othello*," *UTQ* 57, 3 (1988); and "Othello's Occupation," *SS* 24 (1988). I owe a good deal to the readers for the University of Massachusetts Press, David Bevington and Jean E. Howard, who were preternaturally shrewd at discerning weak links in arguments and unusually generous with perceptive advice. Pam Wilkinson, editor *extraordinaire*, and my son Stuart Calderwood, who canvased the manuscript with a meticulosity bordering on the insane, have from many a stylistic blunder freed me, if not foolish notion; and the wit, graciousness, and efficiency of Bruce Wilcox have, as usual, made him the ideal press director to work with. My affection for a friend and admiration for a fine Shakespearean are recorded in the dedication. The text of *Othello* I have used is that of David Bevington in *The Complete Works of Shakespeare*, 3rd edition (Glenview, Ill.: Scott, Foresman, 1980).

The Properties of *Othello*

Introduction

1. Elizabethan Property Lines

This book examines *Othello* from the somewhat unlikely standpoint of property—or rather from the standpoints of property, since the concept is more various than it might seem. Some years ago, for instance, Kenneth Burke argued that in *Othello* Shakespeare dramatizes love in terms of ownership, and even suggested that he might have been influenced by the enclosure movement when he wrote it.[1] A farfetched notion surely, but like most of Burke's notions one that bears looking into. Certainly the sixteenth century left any playwright interested in property a rich legacy of concepts, if only because in that period England was a nation of radically shifting property lines. It is no accident that the term *surveyor*, in the sense of one who marks and divides land, came into currency around 1550. During the previous fifteen years, ever since Cromwell began dissolving the great monastic estates around 1535, about one-sixth of all the land of England had been changing hands by sale or lease; and as the century wore on, surveyors were rarely out of work:

> From the reign of Henry VIII down to the last days of James I, by far the better part of English landed estate changed owners, and in most cases [this property] went from the old nobility by birth and the clergy into the hands of those who possessed money in the period of the Tudors, i.e. principally the merchants and industrialists or the newly created nobility and gentry. . . .[2]

To some extent, then, England owes to the Reformation and the sale of monastic estates the creation of the concept of land as economic property and hence an important step toward the establishment of the market system. "As late as the fourteenth or fifteenth century," Robert L. Heilbroner observes, there was no land, at least in the modern sense of freely salable, rent-producing property. There were lands, of course—estates, manors, and principalities—but these were emphatically not real estate to be bought and sold as the occasion warranted. Such lands formed the core of social life, provided the basis for prestige and status, and constituted the foundation for the military, judicial, and administrative organization of society. Although land was salable under certain conditions (with many strings attached), it was not generally *for sale*. A medieval nobleman in good standing would no more have thought of selling his land than the governor of Connecticut would think of selling a few counties to the governor of Rhode Island.[3]

Thus the dissolution of monastic estates reflected in earthy form the redrawing of spiritual property lines during the Reformation as Anglicans, Catholics, Puritans, and the two and seventy jarring sects among them staked out their claims to Christian demesnes and vigilantly policed their grounds. Property lines did not come into being with the Reformation, of course, but thinking of the religious divisions of the time in this sense makes it easier to see that even secular property lines are inspired by a spiritual drive toward purity and oneness. The English Channel, or the grounds around Hampton Court, or for that matter the brick wall that fronted on New Place, divided the elect from the damned as decidedly as the theological barbed wire between transubstantiation and consubstantiation.

Mentioning the Eucharist has some relevance here because ritual, as Mary Douglas has demonstrated, is a major means of enclosing the pure and repelling the impure. Purity and impurity, hard to imagine as spiritual states, take more convenient material form as the clean and the dirty, and all societies draw lines of demarcation between the two. That is in part how they *become* societies. A sensitivity to dirt is a product of an impulse to order, a desire to establish boundaries and give an identity to those within them.[4] We who do not eat with our dirty left hands (e.g., the Yoruba cult in Nigeria or the Havik Brahmin) belong together; we whose souls have been washed clean by baptism belong together; and we who do not write sloppily, read trash, or use nasty words belong together.

The impulse to order usually collaborates with other impulses. Examples of the kind just mentioned may neatly divide "them" from "us," but the underlying aim is to aggrandize us and denigrate them. The desire for status is at least as instrumental as the desire for order, and since in these cases status is grounded on what is proper to us as opposed to them, an element of possession enters in. "We" possess this color of skin, this language, this noble history, and these social rituals as immutably as we own this land. And we possess them of course because we are clean within, whereas everything about "them" is dirty—their skin, their language, their rituals, their gods, and especially their desire to own what we own and to claim the rights we claim.

Cleanliness then is not only next to godliness, it defines godliness. From this detergent standpoint Elizabethan England was godly indeed, having cleansed itself of a great deal of dirt, especially in the form of Catholics. It was especially important to purge the land of Catholics because Catholics insisted perversely on regarding the English themselves as dirty. "It will be remembered," Richard Marienstras says,

> that in 1570 Pope Pius V had excommunicated Elizabeth. In 1586 Pope Sixtus Quintus offered to pay Philip of Spain one million crowns if he would invade the island. The following year he declared a crusade against England. The Spanish Armada was defeated in 1588 but Spanish ships made another attempt in 1597, and in 1599 they tried to come to the aid of the Irish uprising of Tyrone: a storm—sent by providence, according to the protestants—caused them to fail. In England, to which a number of Jesuit missions had secretly been sent, a series of plots had been discovered: Throckmorton's in 1583, Babington's in 1586, Roderigo Lopez's in 1594. . . . Finally, in 1605, there was the Gunpowder Plot. Threats from within were thus added to threats from without and papists, puritans and foreigners were clearly execrated or suspect. Legislation on treason and religious observance became increasingly specific and inflexible.[5]

Strangers and enemies: the phrase was almost redundant. Even worse was the enemy who looked like a friend—Catholic recusants of the Gunpowder sort, several of whom were Shakespeare's neighbors outside Stratford. But worst of all was the infidel, whom Edward Coke called the "perpetual enemy."[6] The perpetual enemy—an Arab, Jew, African, or Indian—was beyond salvation and outside the law. If he were able and foolish enough to enter England he could not own property or bring any legal action. An infidel prudent enough to remain outside England but foolish enough to remain defenseless could be invaded, robbed, and killed.[7] Killing infidels was virtually a spiritual duty, because whether they knew it or not, they were in the

Devil's camp, devoid of souls, scarcely human, mere brutes. In fact to be in the Devil's camp was almost by definition to be a brute. "It was no accident," Keith Thomas says, "that the symbol of Anti-Christ was the Beast, or that the Devil was regularly portrayed as a mixture of man and animal."[8] It goes without saying that the Devil was also black, with, as Brabantio puts it, "the sooty bosom / Of such a thing as thou."[9]

2. Crossing Borders

Sooty bosoms get us closer to *Othello*, closer certainly to Othello. Of course I am assuming that the Moor *does* have a sooty bosom, although for a long while the theatrical world had its doubts. Actors and critics have made him out to be an Ethiopian, an Abyssinian, a Saracen. Perhaps he could be played as a "tawny Moor" like the Prince of Morocco in *The Merchant of Venice*, or maybe a "veritable negro" as Coleridge held, or even, as a genteel lady from Maryland confidently maintained, a white man. In the Arden edition of the play published in 1958, M. R. Ridley provides his readers with a desperately liberal review of the possibilities that is as offensive as it is unintentionally amusing.[10] He is anxious to assure us that even if Othello were black there is "no reason why he should, even to European eyes, look sub-human"; after all, "One of the finest heads I have ever seen on any human being was that of a negro conductor on an American Pullman car" (p. li). This prepares the fastidious reader for Ridley's conclusion, which is, after a careful weighing of the color options, "that Othello should be imagined in reading, and presented on the stage, as coal-black, a negro, though not at all necessarily of the particular negroid type which Coleridge presumably had in mind when he spoke of a 'veritable negro'" (p. liii).

Othello is black, then. Not, thank God, veritably black, but rather somewhat . . . well, coal-black. However, Ridley judiciously observes,

> if it is thought that such a presentation on the stage will, with a particular type of audience (one with a stronger sense of colour-bar than we may suppose the Elizabethan audience to have had, say an audience in the southern states of America), evoke a reaction of *disgust* at Desdemona rather than one of startled sympathy and admiration, then the presentation had better no doubt be modified, since

that reaction is certainly not what Shakespeare intended and knew would be evoked in his own audience.

"And now," he adds, mopping his forehead, "what of the man himself, whatever his colour?" (p. liv).

But, alas, the man and his color are not so easily parted. The mere presence of the black hero on stage amid white Venetians announces that "our" borders have been crossed by one of "them," especially when "we" are a white English audience whose queen has recently issued an edict demanding the expulsion of blacks from the island.[11] Of course the Queen had her reasons. The most noble was that blacks are, as she wrote, "infidels, having no understanding of Christ or His Gospel."[12] The most obvious was that blacks are black, which means of course that they are from the south. We all know what that means. At least Sir John Davies did when he wrote in *Microcosmos* (1603) that

. . . South-ward, men are cruell, moody, madd,
Hot, blacke, leane, leapers, lustfull, used to vant,
Yet wise in action, sober, fearfull, sad,
If good, most good, if bad exceeding bad.

Among Sir John's contemporaries, Othello the Moor would have triggered off a series of associations. At best, Moors were simply outsiders, the other who is not like us. "The word 'Moor,'" G. K. Hunter notes, "had no clear racial status" to begin with; "its first meaning in the *O.E.D.* is 'Mahomedan,'" which itself meant merely "infidel," "non-Christian," "barbarian."[13] But Othello's blackness would have suggested that he was of the monstrous species *semihomo*, close kin to animals (especially the ape, and hence prone to lusting and leaping) and at the lowest depth of depravity a fellow with Judas and the Prince of Darkness. So the Queen is, as usual, right—the Moor is not our kind; he belongs elsewhere, southward.

On the other hand, it is made quite clear that the Moor is at least somewhat like us in that he is a convert to Christianity.[14] He has crossed spiritual property lines, to be sure, but on a journey that we Christians not only encourage but demand, especially if we Christians in this case are Venetians and a Turkish fleet is sailing for our property in Cyprus, and if the converted infidel is a general whose record of military conquests makes him a likely candidate for doing away with Turks.

From this point of view, Othello clearly belongs in Venice, whatever may be the case in England. But whether he belongs because he is newly washed in the Blood of the Lamb or because he has been swathed in the blood of the Turk, as at Aleppo once, is a question not to be asked. Unfortunately, Iago asks it. As he cynically puts it, Othello can do no wrong in Venice, not at this particular moment anyhow:

> For I do know the state,
> However this [accusation] may gall him with some check,
> Cannot with safety cast him, for he's embarked
> With such loud reason to the Cyprus wars,
> Which even now stands in act, that, for their souls,
> Another of his fathom they have none
> To lead their business. (1.1.149)

Does this mean that the Senate would have sided with Othello even if he *had* made witchcraftily off with Brabantio's daughter? Surely not; who would believe Iago? To be fair, however, Iago's cynicism here may receive confirmation later in a remark of Brabantio's after the Senate has ruled for Othello and the Duke attempts to console him. Brabantio says, with what may well be bitter sarcasm, "I humbly beseech you, proceed to the affairs of state" (1.3.223)—meaning perhaps that the Senate can hardly "proceed" to state affairs because it never left them: the domestic property dispute is merely the Cyprus wars writ small.

Iago and Brabantio make a disconcerting suggestion: when Venetian property rights are threatened, the borders between civilized Christians and barbaric ex-infidels are all too readily erased. Indeed, perhaps they never existed at all; perhaps the barbarian has always been inside the gate of Venice, not in the person of Othello but latent in the civil unconscious. Surely, however, that can't be so. The point is that the Senate *hired* Othello. He is there merely on business—killing business, which happens to be his occupation. You would not expect the "wealthy curled darlings of our nation," as Brabantio calls them (1.2.69), to bloody their doublets and muddy their hose fighting Turks, not when there are, as we Americans say, "freedom fighters" available. Freedom fighters and barbaric mercenaries do for us what we are too civilized to do for ourselves. If we contract with them to kill our enemies, it does not mean that we are alike. It's not analogous, for instance, to Othello's contracting with

Iago to kill *his* enemies: "Now art thou my lieutenant." Still, when the Senate hired Othello, did someone say "Now art thou our general"? And did he reply "I am your own forever"?

If so, that was different. And if there appears to be a parallel between the Senate's hiring a barbarian to kill Turks when Venice's property is threatened and the Moor's own murderousness when he thinks *his* marital property has been stolen, well, that's different too.

As all of this suggests, the presence of this particular Moor produces some unconventional loops and squiggles in the property lines of white society in Venice, very much as casting a Moor as tragic hero instead of as villain (like Aaron in *Titus Andronicus*) redraws some generic lines in the Globe. But the real surprise is finding the source of evil not in the devilish-looking black stranger but in the honest-looking white citizen of Venice—not the enemy outside, like the Turks, or the stranger inside, like the Moor, but the enemy who has always been inside, the enemy who is one of us.

Still, who really owns Iago; who will own up to owning him? Clearly Venice, insofar as he is a Venetian citizen; and yet, as the "I am your own forever" line indicates, Othello owns him too. Or, on the other hand, is it Iago who owns Othello? Iago may not be the Devil, but if he is even a peripheral member of the tribe of hell then his business is to reclaim infidels to the demonic faith. Does the blackness of this ex-infidel suggest that those whom the Devil marks for his own cannot truly change their color, baptism notwithstanding? Brabantio would readily agree. If Desdemona sees "Othello's visage in his mind," Brabantio sees the Devil's there, or at least that of a man who has practiced a bafflingly diabolical witchcraft on his daughter. If so, then Brabantio's daughter is strangely and variously possessed by the Moor.

3. Owning

If possession can take several forms, so can property. Consider Cassio, whom Iago declares to be "a proper man" (1.3.394). Editors gloss *proper* here as "handsome" to remind us that Cassio is a likely object of jealousy, although Iago also sneeringly means, no doubt, that he is an excellent man, a capital man—in short, a popinjay.[15] Surely Cassio is proper also in virtue of possessing the Venetian social graces. Unfortunately he possesses more of them than may be proper, for "he hath," Iago adds, "a person and a smooth dispose / To be suspected." Sure enough, on Desdemona's arrival in Cyprus, so smooth is Cassio's dispose that his courtesies suggest more than courtesy to Iago:

> He takes her by the palm. Ay, well said, whisper. With as little a web
> as this will I ensnare as great a fly as Cassio. Ay, smile upon her, do; I
> will gyve thee in thine own courtship.   (2.1.166–69)

Thus Cassio outdoes himself in propriety, enabling Iago to undo him later. Yet in the end it is the proper Cassio, suspected of improperly taking Othello's place with Desdemona, who does take his place as military ruler of Cyprus and even "seize[s] upon the fortunes of the Moor, / For they succeed on [him]" (5.2.375).

Something improper, it seems, is going on not only with the Moor's property but also with the concept of property in *Othello*. A kind of semantic incest seems to take place within the family of terms comprised by *property, propriety, appropriate*, and *proprietor*. *Property* has both the outward sense of "things owned" and the inward sense of "a defining quality, characteristic, or attribute"; *appropriate* is both a verb and an adjective; and *propriety* is the province of *proprietors*. That is, the defining property of propriety may be the possession of property itself, inasmuch as propriety was once simply the standards of conduct of the propertied classes, much as nobility, Nietzsche pointed out, was once the exclusive possession of *the* nobility.[16] Again, the inward properties that define someone are themselves defined by the outward properties he or she possesses—if we apply the principle that you are what you own.

What separates this family of terms from others, however, is the importance of possession. Underlying all is the English word *proper* in its adopted Latin sense of *proprius*, "one's (or its) own, personal, particular." At bottom, to appropriate, to be propertied, to be proper, even to *be* at all, is to possess. Thus Diana in *All's Well* speaks postpositively to Bertram of his "own proper wisdom" (4.2.49); Ariel talks of men "who hang and drown / Their proper selves" (3.3.59); and Hamlet complains that Claudius has angled "for my proper life" (5.2.66). A life or a self is not just something that "is" but something you "have" or "own." Everyone is a capitalist when it comes to proper selves and lives; they are the indispensable collateral for all subsequent possessings.

And why those subsequent possessings of property? Well, apart from the practical advantages, perhaps because they function as an economic substitute for the fusion of self with nature in prelapsarian times. Anthropologists tell us that archaic peoples did not conceive of the self in terms of "inner" and "outer"; there was no boundary between consciousness and the "objective" world, it was all one.[17] The breakdown of this primal unity into subjective and objective entailed a divorce from the world but also a birth of the self. In place of a deep sense of belonging, economic man substitutes owning and possessing. Property in the form of land and animals may be merely the fragments of a dismembered natural world, but it is all that remains to mediate between us and an irrecoverable past. However as parts and parcels of nature become *mine* within an economic system that encourages others to make *mine* into *theirs,* property becomes self-alienating in Marx's sense; and by the time it has come to include not just parts of nature but also manufactured goods, then its shadowy role in an attenuated communion between humans and nature is erased, and it becomes world alienating as well.

Again, property is an attempt to materialize time and lend an air of permanence to our transient identities. To possess a diamond is not merely to publicize the size of your bank account but also to enhance your personal value by participating in its enduring brilliance. The golden crown of England wears away far more slowly than the royal heads it adorns, but if one of those heads is yours, even for a short while, you insert yourself into the eternal round of English greatness. As externalized identity, a visual sign of the self, property can be an ennobling monument that allows you to transcend death before death. With each thing he touches, Midas turns more enduringly gold himself, a time-defying Ozymandias before his time. But of course Ozymandias testifies eloquently to the fact that property is itself transient. Before Lear's eyes a hundred bodyguards shrivel into an O without a circle. One minute you own a palace and have a guest list of thousands; the next, Timon discovers, you are digging for roots and possessed by fleas. Othello knows the feeling.

In this light we see Othello's loss of Desdemona at its furthest symbolic reach. For of course Othello, like Shakespeare's countrymen, indeed like Shakespeare himself, is a capitalist in marriage. Monogamy is a matter of staking out property rights, and the ban on divorce in Shakespeare's day was an endorsement of the irrevocable privacy of the property so staked out. The function of marriage was patrimonial business; its primary aim was to "ensure the perpetuation of the family and its property" by securing financial and ter-

ritorial advantages and producing a male heir.[18] Shakespeare often
depicts children as the profits generated by sexual transactions in the
marriage bed.[19]

Even love has its element of ownership in the ecstatic *Mine!*
that rewards the smitten for going for weeks on end without food,
sleep, and other prerequisites of sentient life. This erotic *mine*, which
may range from cherishing to ravishing, stands opposed to the *yours!*
of *agape* or *caritas*, the Christian's love of God and fellow Christians.
Somewhere in between is the aesthetic experience, usually held to be
a moment of arrest in the presence of a beauty to which you can say
neither *yours* nor *mine*, though of course you can own the canvas,
stone, or book itself. Desdemona, whose love for Othello seems about
one part *eros* to three parts *agape*, seems capable of calling forth any of
the three feelings from others, but her fate—discussed in the following chapter—is to fall in her husband's imagination from the divine
to the profane, from a "most blessed condition" to the status not
merely of marital property but of common whorish goods.

Perhaps my most consistent interest in this book is in the
notion of property as identity. At the end of the play the suicidal
Othello calls on his audience to "Speak of me as I am," very much as
the dying Hamlet calls on Horatio to tell his "story to the yet unknowing world." Both men are "storied" heroes, alike in being composed
and preserved by words. But when Horatio comes to tell Hamlet's
story, he will have little to say about property, whereas those who tell
Othello's story will find it crucial to recovering the meaning of the
Moor.

Recovering meanings is of course a matter of recovering distinctions. Othello is a man of distinction in both senses of the word—
a very visible black African outsider in Venice, but also an aristocrat
who "fetches his life and being / From men of royal siege" and a
general whose services to the signiory can out-tongue complaints
(1.2.18 ff.). As these quotes suggest, at this point Othello responds
readily and confidently to his own later request to "speak of me as I
am." It takes an entire play before Hamlet can stand up and say
"This is I, Hamlet, the Dane," whereas in fewer than five or six lines
from his first entrance Othello boasts that he will not boast that he is
Othello, son of kings, valued general of Venice, and a man fortunate
in that "[his] parts, [his] title, and [his] perfect soul / Shall manifest
[him] rightly." This series of possessive pronouns testifies to a hero
who is in full possession of his attributes, a lord and owner of his self.

And yet before a seeming two days are out this same man will lose his parts when he falls into a fit, his title of commander of Cyprus when he is replaced by Cassio, and the perfection of his soul when he murders his wife. By that time, of course, he is not the same man at all.

By "my perfect soul" Othello probably means completeness of self, perfect in the sense in which Macbeth uses the term on learning that Fleance has escaped:

> I had else been perfect,
> Whole as the marble, founded as the rock. (3.4.21)

Macbeth spent an entire play chasing that "else" that would have made him perfect; Othello, it seems, has already found it by the time he comes on stage. In the face of Brabantio's charges, he is totally self-possessed. But why? What does he have that Macbeth lacks?

The ambitious Macbeth tries to complete himself by violence, by killing a king to become a king. But the murderous deed perversely remains undone, and he, therefore, so unperfected and incomplete that the meanings he sought dribble away at last in idiotic syllables. Othello, on the other hand, completes himself not by killing kings but by loving and marrying Desdemona. Unfortunately, somewhat like Macbeth's murder, Othello's marriage begets consequences, thanks to Iago, that must be trammeled up before it and the Moor will be perfected. Brabantio's charges must be answered. But who will speak for the black stranger in Venice? Actually, he has several advocates. First, his own services:

> Let [Brabantio] do his spite.
> My services which I have done the signiory
> Shall out-tongue his complaints. (1.2.17)

Second, he himself: "Say it, Othello," says the Duke, and Othello says it so grandly—"it" being the manner of his wooing the magnifico's daughter—that the Duke replies "I think this tale would win my daughter too." However, Brabantio's charges are not answered definitively until Desdemona comes forth: "I pray you, hear her speak," her father says. What he hears is that the Moor is neither a bewitcher nor a freebooter but his daughter's legitimate husband and lord to whose "utmost pleasure" her "heart's subdued."

Ultimately, then, Desdemona speaks for Othello in Venice. It is her testimony, her capacity to say "I saw Othello's visage in his mind," that renders Othello's inward virtues visible to the Senate. It is not his parts, his title, and his perfect soul that manifest him truly enough to exonerate him, it is Desdemona.

Broadly conceived, Desdemona's testifying for Othello before the Senate illustrates the plight of the stranger in Venice. His problem is semiotic. What outward signs can truly betoken the inward signified of his noble selfhood? Until now he has defined himself in terms of his military occupation, for the loss of which he reserves one of his most sorrowing speeches. He is, it seems, what he does, and what he does is make war, for Venice. Thus his status is ambiguous. Venice is not Sparta, where warfare is intrinsically valuable and warriors are honored as patriots. Venice, popular symbol of Renaissance mercantilism and avarice, makes money, not war; and Othello is a mercenary, not a patriot—a hired gun, albeit of the most noble and romantic sort.[20] In Venice, where magnificoes like Brabantio testify to the efficacy of Iago's advice to "put money in thy purse," a man takes his identity not so much from what he does as from what he owns. Property is the clothing of the self; it prices and displays one's inner worth.

Measured by such values, "an extravagant and wheeling stranger / Of here and everywhere" (1.1.137) is severely disadvantaged. The Moor's deeds are in the past, his friends are few, his house at the moment is an inn, and, worst of all, his mind and virtues are hidden beneath the surface appearance of a Moor, a blackamoor. To be a black in Venice is to be a stranger, wherever you come from, even if you are a Venetian. Othello's case may seem unique, but the mirror he looks in reflects a universally human face. We are all trapped by accident inside bodies that misrepresent us, making us strangers in Venice to everyone but the Desdemonas who love us. Nevertheless, as a black foreigner Othello has a special need to ex-press his inward self. A major way of accomplishing this is to tell the story of his life to Brabantio, to tell it again to Desdemona, and then, when it becomes apparent that she loves him for the dangers he has survived, "upon this hint" to speak for her hand. Then she becomes his, a lovely objective correlative to his nobility. In her shining beauty and virtue, his inward self is reflected.

In other words Othello seems an allegorist of sorts. As one of the least sentient of Shakespeare's tragic heroes, he attempts to come to terms with what is within him not by introspection, like Hamlet, Brutus, and Macbeth, but by allegorical extroversion. After all, if the playwright denies him the right to soliloquize, conferring all inward

speech on his enemy Iago, what is he to do? He will let Desdemona
speak for him. To make her his own is not merely to cherish her as a
woman and a wife but also, in a sublime way, to take Iago's advice and
put money in his purse. Not of course in any mercenary sense;
Othello is hardly in pursuit of a dowry or, as Iago puts it, a "land-
carrack." Rather he seeks to project his inner properties, his nobility,
into outer property, the beautiful and virtuous Desdemona. Unfortunately this entails a certain risk. To externalize your self in the form of
property, especially in such beloved property as Desdemona, is in
some degree to wear your pulsing heart upon your sleeve where daws
may peck at it. And one daw in particular has a very sharp beak.

4. Roderigo's Dispossessions

Before seeing what happens to Othello when he puts money in
his marital purse, let us see what happens to the man to whom Iago
gave that advice, Roderigo. His experience suggests how important
the notion of property is in *Othello*.

Roderigo is interesting because he does not exist in Cinthio's
story; Shakespeare invented him. To what end? Apparently to serve
as a kind of foolish metaphor for Othello. As Iago's gull, Roderigo
testifies to the manipulative skills of the ancient, he forecasts (and
helps make credible) the deception of the Moor, and he dignifies the
Moor's fate by contrast. Moreover, as a man of property he helps
illuminate a dimension of Othello's experience that is somewhat
shadowed from our view by the romanticism of the opening act.

Roderigo's case suggests that we should distinguish between
real and monetary property. In Shakespeare's time "real" property,
and land in particular, was in fact more valuably real than any other.
But as I have mentioned, the sixteenth century brought about an
extraordinary reorganization of property lines, and the period from
1585 to 1606 in particular saw so many sales of manorial holdings at
net losses that Lawrence Stone says "one may reasonably talk about a
financial crisis of the aristocracy."[21]

This crisis extends all the way to Venice, thanks to Iago, whose
freedom with Roderigo's purse compels the lord to sell his land to
purchase Desdemona (1.3.382). "Thus," Iago says, "do I ever make
my fool my purse" (383). Later, when his efforts to help Iago disgrace
Cassio result in his being, as he ruefully reports, "exceedingly well
cudgeled" by the drunken lieutenant, Roderigo declares an end to his
speculations on the sexual market. "With no money at all and a little

more wit," he says "[I will] return again to Venice" (2.3.359–62). However, Iago predictably talks him into raising his hopes even higher and opening his purse even wider until at last, thoroughly cudgeled financially, he demands either a return of his jewels or "satisfaction" from Iago (4.2.198–202). Iago assures him that he "shall be satisfied" (246), and ultimately puts an end to his desires by putting an end to him.

Roderigo's fate clarifies Othello's insofar as they are both property owners. Roderigo is a Venetian gentleman and appropriately therefore a landowner. The virtue of land is that it is truly private property, reliably bound to its owner by contract. Money, on the other hand, is common. My land is mine, and yours is yours, and each differs from the other much as our proper selves differ from one another. But we both carry the same coins in our pockets. The commonest man can carry a noble or even a crown in his pocket, and, handy-dandy, even nobles and kings are sometimes obliged to carry pennies. And because pennies can be exchanged for nobles or crowns and vice versa, money is subtly subversive of the social differences it helps create. Like the Colt .44, which settled so many differences in the old West, money is an equalizer.[22]

Moreover, like the Colt .44, money makes for sudden and transient encounters. In a landowning feudal society an oath of fealty binds lord and vassal for life, but in a mercantile society of the sort England was becoming in Shakespeare's time, this oath was replaced by contracts calling for the fulfillment of particular promises by a specified time, after which the various parties went their ways, as Iago goes his way after terminating affairs with the hapless Roderigo.[23]

Land, then, is honest in the double sense of being true and chaste; mother earth makes a man a good wife—fecund, loyal, enduring. But money is a strumpet; and the quick cash transaction at the brothel epitomizes the casual relationships it promotes. (It is appropriate that Roderigo is a landowner during the time he seeks to wed Desdemona, before the play opens, and a moneyowner during the time he seeks simply to bed her.) That money brings little in the way of loyalty is clear from the opening lines of the play when Roderigo complains that his purse has failed not only to buy him Desdemona but even to purchase Iago's intelligence:

> Tush, never tell me! I take it much unkindly
> That thou, Iago, who hast had my purse
> As if the strings were thine, shouldst know of this.

Such an opening speech suggests that property lines will be hard to draw in this play. If the purse is in Roderigo's hand but the strings are in Iago's, to whom does it belong? In the long run, we can be sure, purse, strings, and contents will all belong to Iago; but for the moment everything seems common property in a villainous parody of free-sharing friendship. The villainy extends to Desdemona as well, since in the glitter of this monetary imagery she figures as merely a piece of flashy goods. In fact for 170 lines, until we discover she is married, the only view we have of her and Othello is summed up in Roderigo's "What a fortune does the thick-lips owe, / If he can carry it thus!" (67).

As I suggested earlier, for Othello to make Desdemona his own is in a sublime way to take Iago's advice and put money in his purse. Roderigo makes the point crudely. For in following Iago's advice he assumes that if he can put enough money in his purse, then he may be able to make Desdemona his sexual purse. But the question that arises with respect to Roderigo's purse—Who owns it?—arises again with respect to Desdemona as purse—Who owns her? Othello has legal title, but that, as Iago soon makes clear, is no guarantee of private possession. Like Iago with Roderigo, Cassio may have the strings to Othello's wifely purse. In which case the Moor may well follow Roderigo into bankruptcy.

Thus Roderigo's descent from propertied aristocrat to impoverished fool mirrors Othello's descent from husband to apparent cuckold as Desdemona falls from wife to whore. Iago's advice to Roderigo proves predictively apt. The route to Desdemona's bed may not be through Roderigo's purse, but for Othello in the Brothel Scene it seems that way. At any rate he subscribes to the Iago principle when he says "There's money for your pains," and puts coins for Desdemona in Emilia's palm. Like Roderigo's lands, Othello's wife has been converted to cash. But then, as Iago would be quick to point out, whorish wives and cuckolded husbands are common as coin in Venice. Unfortunately, in this play the price of becoming common is death.

5. Previews

Liberally construed, the concept of property ramifies in all directions in *Othello*. Shakespeare was interested not only in masculine property rights in marriage but in masculine properties as well—in what it takes to be a man. Iago, ever solicitous of Othello's dignity, says "Would you would bear your fortune like a man!" and Othello replies "A horned man's a monster and a beast" (4.1.61).[24] Iago then begins another speech by saying "Good sir, be a man" and adds that

> There's millions now alive
> That nightly lie in those unproper beds
> Which they dare swear peculiar.

If to "be a man" instead of a "monster and a beast" is to be one who nightly lies in a properly peculiar bed, then it seems that men are desperately dependent on their wives for their identities. Shakespeare carries this beyond metaphor into a concept of identity analogous to Lacan's "mirror stage," a subject considered both optically and linguistically in Chapter 3.

No one who has heard Othello is likely to forget that he is propertied with a voice and a style distinctively his own. This evokes some speculations about the nature of Othello's speech, its self-fashioning powers, and its vulnerability to Iago's deconstructive maneuvers. At its furthest reach, the concept of property extends well beyond Roderigo's lands and purse to include Shakespeare's rather capacious literary purse also. If we can ask who owns Iago or Desdemona, we can also ask who owns *Othello*. Does Shakespeare hold title to the play outright, free and clear, or should we institute a title search? To some extent, the answer depends on the properties of the play itself. One of these is repetition, or as Othello calls it, iterance. Irascibly, he demands of Emilia what has been demanded of most wives at one time or another, "What needs this iterance, woman?" The question seems of sufficient importance, and the instances of iterance of sufficient number in the play, for me to enlarge at some length on Emilia's rather uninformative answer. But ultimately only Iago can answer Othello's questions, or our own, and of course Iago is even less forthcoming than his wife. Thus a final chapter addresses his villainies and his motives from a metadramatic perspective, attending to his role as interior playwright, master plotter, and johannes factotum of the theater, and suggesting why his taciturn "What you know, you know" will not prevent books like this, however unknowing, from continuing to supply definitive answers for him.

II

Property, Violence, and Women

1. Sublimation

This chapter is occasioned in part by the Sagittary. Near the end of the opening scene, Brabantio, having been aroused from bed by the news of his daughter's apparent abduction, cries for tapers and prepares to go in search of Othello. Iago, thinking it tactically advisable to slip away in order to be found with Othello, tells Roderigo "Lead to the Sagittary the raised search, / And there I will be with him" (1.1.160). And off he goes to the Sagittary, which editors usually identify as an inn. Why should an inn the audience never sees require a name? Perhaps to emphasize Othello's somewhat transient status as a mercenary in Venice, the "unhoused free condition" (1.2.26) which he is surrendering in exchange for a wife and presumably in the future a home of some sort. Further on, however, the name appears again. When Brabantio brings his charges before the Senate, Othello replies by saying "Send for the lady to the Sagittary, / And let her speak of me before her father" (1.3.117).

This second appearance of the name sent me in some puzzlement from one text of *Othello* to another until with some relief I found, not an answer, but what is usually just as satisfying—shared confusion. For in his edition of the play, the distinguished Irish editor Bertram O'States comments a bit testily:

> This is the second time the name "Sagittary" has appeared (see 1.1.160). As a result I have spent I do not care to say how many hours going through old editions of the play, letters in the *Times Literary Supplement,* and items in *Notes and Queries* and the "Notes" section of the *Shakespeare Quarterly* without coming upon anything that makes even a gesture toward a relevant answer to this question. I can, however, definitively state that the proper spelling of the word is *Sagittary,* as in Quarto 2, that it has nothing to do with the Arsenal

where military officers stayed in Venice or with the Frezzaria (the street of the arrow-makers), but that it very likely refers to an inn of Shakespeare's imagining. Still, what is the point?[1]

Well, what *is* the point? Just the question we so often ask when faced with suspiciously conspicuous irrelevancies in Shakespeare; when we encounter for instance a mysterious "Claudio" at a rather tense moment in *Hamlet* (4.7.40) or an odd argument about "widow Dido" and the location of Tunis in *The Tempest* (2.1.67–85). These slight distractions give us pause. Has Shakespeare given us a nudge and a wink? Perhaps we should take a closer look.[2]

Taking a closer look at the Sagittary will hardly revolutionize our interpretations of *Othello*, but it may suggest a view of Othello's courtship and marriage that lends a kind of backdoor credence to honest Iago. As everyone knows, Iago reads an obscene misogynistic interpretation into the action of Act 1. Before Othello arrives on stage Iago has already imposed this view of the marriage on Roderigo, Brabantio, and the audience as well. Of course Shakespeare guarantees that we are not wholly taken in; he has already had Iago declare his hatred of the Moor and his villainous intent to serve his turn upon him. Iago thinks he is setting up the Moor, when in fact he is himself being set up by the playwright. Othello comes on stage and simply blows him and his interpretation away by force of personal presence—and of course by telling the Senate a story about his storytelling courtship. One interpretation drives out another. When the Senate renders its decision, foulness is purged by nobility, disorder yields to order, love is ratified by law, and the audience is given some cause to hope later on, as events take a tragic turn, that a similar reversal will occur to thwart Iago and rescue the hero and heroine.

That makes the play sound a bit like *The Perils of Pauline*. What it should be likened to, however, at least in its opening act, is *Civilization and Its Discontents*, because it so clearly illustrates Freud's argument that civilization entails the suppression of the barbaric in the interests of the sublime. The barbaric is not, we discover, an attribute of Othello but a product of Iago's vengeful imagination. When the Senate endorses Othello and licenses his marriage, Iago's interpretation of things is heaped with shame and driven from Venice—a kind of scapegoat ritual in which hermeneutic dirt is swept away, purifying the city. Iago is not ridden out of town on a rail, but his views are muted and repressed, driven from the public streets, the theatrical consciousness, down into the theatrical version of the unconscious—the "silence" of the soliloquy with which he concludes the first act.

So nobility and love triumph despite Iago. Of course they also triumph in part *because* of him, because without his opposition they should not have shone so gloriously. He ushers Othello and Desdemona to greatness the way Falstaff and his low-life companions usher a suddenly effulgent Prince Hal to his coronation. But unlike Falstaff, who is banished and soon dies so that King Harry can have the stage of England to himself, Iago not only reappears to have the last word in Act 1 but also his earlier words, though gone, are not forgotten. Against our will perhaps, he reminds us that sublimation is accomplished by repression, and that a romantic elopement may be what it is by virtue of not being what it might have been, a barbaric seizure and rape of another man's property. Even though we reject Iago's interpretation of the action, as the Senate does, we may still register its inappropriateness as a kind of irritable trace or shadow of the "discontent" that attends civilization in Venice.

2. Property as Prize

The effect of opening the play with Iago and Roderigo and their talk about money and marriage is, among other things, to define Desdemona as a prize to be contested for and won. The fact that Othello has now got title to her does not conclude the contest but only whets Roderigo's interest once Iago holds out further hope. From this standpoint, whatever her intrinsic worth or economic promise, Desdemona is valuable by virtue of the fact that she is competed for. As René Girard has stressed, value is conferred by desire, and especially by mimetic desire in which I want what you want because you want it.[3] And Desdemona is wanted by everyone, by Roderigo, Brabantio, Othello, "Cassio," and even by Iago himself, Iago claims, not wanting to leave a promising motive lying about unused.

However, one of the curiosities of the first act is that it focuses as much on Othello's besting of Brabantio as it does on his winning of Desdemona. When Othello replies to Brabantio's charges by saying to the senators "That I have ta'en away this old man's daughter, / It is most true" (1.3.80), the phrase "this old man's" may be innocent, but it also may suggest that the taking away has capped a kind of contest in virility and strength. Iago put it more crudely when he taunted Brabantio:

Your heart is burst, you have lost half your soul.
Even now, now, very now, an old black ram
Is tupping your white ewe.   (1.1.88)

What is interesting about this speech, as Michael Neill observes, is
that it "presents the abduction of a daughter as though it were an act
of adultery."[4]

In other words, here and elsewhere in this act there are implications of a violence at work beneath the forms of civilized order in
Venice, a violence that centers in property as much as in sex. This is
suggested not merely by Iago's remarks but by the ominous reports
about the Turkish invasion that swirl around the Senate. For the
sudden courtship of Desdemona by Othello has its public correlative
in the threatened capture of Cyprus by the Turks. Just as the barba-
rous Turks threaten to seize the Venetian property of Cyprus, so
Othello has seized the Brabantian property of Desdemona. The parallel reinforces Brabantio's charges of thievery, which characterize
Othello as a pirate who has boarded a "land-carrack" (1.2.50), made
off with the magnifico's "jewel" (1.3.198), and "stowed" her away
for his own barbaric uses (1.2.63). For even if Othello is a Christian,
not a Turk—though by the end of the play he will portray himself as
one—his blackness is a constant reminder that he was not to the
Christian manner born. Brabantio's charges of witchcraft suggest
how easily in his view the Christian convert may revert to diabolical
heathenism. "Bond slaves and pagans shall our statesmen be," he
forecasts, if Othello is not checked (1.2.100). Even if Othello is not an
infidel, he is an outsider, admittedly ill-schooled in Venetian manners, a rough soldier used to fighting and seizing. In this case he did
not simply charge Turkishly into Brabantio's home and carry off a
maiden but submitted his desires to the shows of courtship.

Not that Othello is deviously using Christianity and civilized
behavior as a stalking-horse for a barbaric assault. It is less a matter of
individual psychology, of discovering a set of secret and somewhat
Iago-like motives governing the conduct of a pseudo-noble Moor,
than a matter of seeing something in the psychology of the text, a
pattern of suggestion that underlies action, as against character, and
constitutes a kind of thematic undertow tugging against the idealistic
current of this opening act.[5] In this connection the mysteriously
twice-named Sagittary may prove instructive. For the name derives
from Shakespeare, not Othello, and inscribes its meaning in the text,
not in the character of the hero.

But just what does it inscribe? For one thing, the image of humans, especially the human male, as centaur. For Sagittarius, the zodiacal archer, is pictorially represented as a centaur, and the centaur perfectly illustrates man's ambiguous relationship to nature. For instance, as Erich Fromm puts it—

> Man transcends all other life because he is, for the first time, *life aware of itself*. Man is *in* nature, subject to its dictates and accidents, yet he transcends nature because he lacks the unawareness which makes the animal a part of nature—as one with it. Man is confronted with the frightening conflict of being the prisoner of nature, yet being free in his thoughts; being a part of nature, and yet to be as it were a freak of nature; being neither here nor there. Human self-awareness has made man a stranger in the world, separate, lonely, and frightened.[6]

Frightened perhaps most of all by the thought that we are inextricably caught in our animal nature. The centaur emblematizes that fear in the image of the higher human form straining, one may imagine, to free itself from its brute origins; while at the same time, from the brutish perspective, it suggests an atavistic longing to be reabsorbed into and identified with all that savage equine power. "To Renaissance humanists," James Hall says, "[the centaurs] personified man's lower, partly animal, nature and might be contrasted with the higher wisdom symbolized by Minerva."[7]

That some such feelings underlay the symbolism of the centaurs is suggested also by the fact that their most infamous mythological act was the attempt by Eurytus to carry off and rape Hippodamia during her wedding to Pirithous.[8] This outrage set off the battle of the Lapithae and the centaurs which Ovid retails at such length in the *Metamorphoses* (12:210–535) and to which Shakespeare refers in *Titus Andronicus* (5.2.203) and *A Midsummer Night's Dream* (5.1.4). To the Renaissance as well as to the ancients, the driving off of the centaurs by Theseus and the Greeks was a locus classicus representing the victory of civilization over barbarism.[9]

How ironic then that the shift from Scene 1 to Scene 2 entails the on-stage replacement of Brabantio's house, representative of Venetian civilization, by the Sagittary, with its centaurian sign hanging over the door.[10] Victories over barbarism, it seems, are hard won and easily lost again, as Kurtz discovers when he travels upriver into the heart of darkness. Thus in the darkness with which *Othello* opens, barbarism seems to have reclaimed its own from the very center of civilization. The victory goes to the centaurs, inasmuch as the Moor successfully makes off with Desdemona to the Sagittary, where we have a union consummated (if indeed it is) quite literally under the sign of the centaur. In the myth, the institution of marriage is pitted against the barbarism of abduction and rape. In the play, the appearance of a thievish abduction and rape in the first two scenes is supplanted in the third scene by the civilized reality of marriage— brought about, however, by a nocturnal elopement and a surreptitious wedding that partly defy marital conventions in Venice even as they partly defer to them.

Shakespeare puts his audience in a difficult position here. He invokes a barbaric mythological incident to reinforce Iago's view of the elopement, and then tells us to dismiss all that and substitute instead a romantic marriage of a splendidly independent and idealistic couple. What are we to think? That the romantic individuality that defies conventions is a charming but dangerous aspect of a forbidden barbarism to which we are all secretly attracted? That even the civilized institution of marriage is grounded in the primitive masculine desire to conquer and possess? If so, then the location of the Sagittary seems additionally meaningful. Its being situated in Venice suggests that barbarity is not exclusive to Othello, that all men, even Venetians, are centaurian. Thus its presence turns an ironic light on Brabantio's outraged reply to Roderigo: "What tell'st thou me of robbing? This is Venice; / My house is not a grange" (1.1.106)—or, as it were, "What tell'st thou me of centaurs? This is Venice!" At the same time the fact that the Sagittary is an inn would seem to typify sublimation in Venice, the sort that produces Brabantio's "This is Venice"; for inns cater not to citizens but to strangers and passers-through, to moorish generals and others whose alien and primitive natures lodge more naturally under the sign of the beast.

The puzzling presence of the Sagittary, then, underscores the fact that what the marriage of Othello and Desdemona is proved *not to be* has been asserted so graphically as to resist erasure. Crude images of old black rams tupping white ewes under the sign of the centaur do not readily wash away despite the sponging motions of the Senate Scene. Nor, even more pointedly, does Iago's warning to Brabantio that "you'll have your daughter covered with a Barbary horse; you'll have coursers for cousins and gennets for germans (1.1.111), which attributes to Othello a barbaric equine lechery that couples naturally with the salacious suggestiveness of the Sagittary. In this context Iago's exhortation to Brabantio, "Arise! Arise!" (1.1.90), lends priapic overtones to the contest that concludes with Othello's "I have ta'en away this old man's daughter." (This is not to cast incestuous aspersions on Brabantio, much less on Desdemona, but merely to remark that pulse of sexual possessiveness that so often seems to quicken proprietorial desire in Shakespeare's fathers, for whom the late-arriving archetype is the secretly incestuous King Antiochus in *Pericles*.)

Yet courtship, we have to keep telling ourselves, is not conquest, and marriage is not rape. Instead of physically seizing Desdemona, Othello tells her romantic *stories* about strange places and barbaric creatures and indeed one in which Othello, not Desdemona, is "taken by the insolent foe / And sold to slavery." Desdemona is ravished not by Othello but by his rhetoric; for she "bade me," he says, "if I had a friend that loved her, / I should but teach him how to tell my story, / And that would woo her."

True, all true, and yet . . .

3. Property as Identity

The aura of contest and competition at the opening of the play suggests an impulse not merely to win a wife but to defeat an opponent as well. The first hint of this is Iago's warning to Othello about Brabantio's proud status in Venice:

> Be assured of this,
> That the magnifico is much beloved,
> And hath in his effect a voice potential
> As double as the Duke's. He will divorce you,
> Or put upon you what restraint and grievance
> The law, with all his might to enforce it on,
> Will give him cable. (1.2.11–17)

Othello responds as if to a challenge, trumpeting his credentials and his eagerness to enter the lists:

> Let him do his spite.
> My services which I have done the signiory
> Shall out-tongue his complaints. 'Tis yet to know—
> Which, when I know that boasting is an honor,
> I shall promulgate—I fetch my life and being

> From men of royal siege, and my demerits
> May speak unbonneted to as proud a fortune
> As this that I have reached.

It's a question of status, then—of whether Othello weighs as much in Venice as Brabantio and therefore merits his daughter. He says he does. His status comes not from economic property, however, as the magnifico's does, not from deeds and titles to lands and manors, but from deeds and titles of a nearer sort—his martial "services" and royal ancestry. With these, he can claim further title to "as proud a fortune / As this that I have reached." The stress here should fall on the adjective, not the noun; the riches he has won are aesthetic and spiritual—Othello is a mercenary in war, not in love. To win Desdemona is to acquire an external property that will reflect his internal worth: he will be what he owns. But at this point in the play we cannot tell whether he owns Desdemona or not, only that he has her, and although possession may be nine-tenths of the law, it is not all of it. He could still be, as far as we can tell, the thief Iago and Brabantio proclaim him to be.

Thanks to Iago, the first act reverberates with the notion of thievery. His stress on it lends the concept special interest. Thievery, one could argue, is a perverted form of communication. Instead of a sender, a message, and a receiver, it features an owner, a property, and a thief. The obvious focus in Act I is on Desdemona as the desirable property and Othello as the suggestively centaurian thief whose value will be enhanced by what he steals. Sometimes, however, what is stolen may be less important than who it is stolen from, in this case Brabantio.

Communication entails a willingness to place private property (meanings) in the public domain. Thieves, however, are not usually utopian communists; they believe in private property. If everything were held in common, there would be no virtue in stealing. No one steals whores for instance; there are no deadbolt locks in the hold-door trade, as the Mistresses Quickly and Overdone can attest. Hippodamia, on the other hand, is a prize to take a centaur's eye not despite but because she is on the verge of becoming the marital property of Pirithous. What is Eurytus's real motive at the feast of the Lapithae, to steal Hippodamia or to steal *from* Pirithous? And what does it mean to steal *from* someone? Does it imply malice or perhaps a perverted kind of love? In any event, an imaginative thief may find the thrills of thievery enhanced if he steals not so much to acquire property as to acquire an owner's "properties." In the following passage, for instance, Jean Genet records his feelings during the act of burglary:

> I do not exactly reflect on the owner of the place, but all my gestures evoke him insofar as they see him. I am steeped in an idea of property while I loot property. I re-create the absent proprietor. He lives, not facing me, but about me. He is a fluid element which I breathe, which enters me, which inflates my lungs. The decision [to leave] is born when the apartment contains no more secret spots, when I have taken the proprietor's place.[11]

With thieves like Genet about, to be an owner is more perilous than it would seem. By externalizing your personal value in the form of property you risk becoming a piece of property yourself. From the thief's perspective, the proverbial "You are what you own" becomes "You are what the owner of what you steal is." Stealing his victim's possessions, Genet steals his soul as well, absorbing his mana in an act of economic cannibalism.[12] He steals not so much from malice or envy as from a desire to communicate with, to become like; not so much to acquire property as to supplement his self.

Othello's method of acquiring status in Venice bears some resemblance to Genet's. After all, it was not Desdemona he first courted but Brabantio:

> Her father loved me, oft invited me;
> Still questioned me the story of my life,
> From year to year . . .   (1.3.130)

Like Genet, the unpropertied Othello enters the house of the magnifico, steeps himself in the ambience of wealth, status, and the love of the "much-beloved," and at last steals his most valuable property. In fact, when Iago describes this process to Brabantio as "an old black ram / . . . tupping your white *ewe*," after having just said, "*you* have lost half your soul," the pun on *ewe/you* suggests that the theft of Desdemona is a rape of Brabantio, not of course with Genet's homosexual intent but surely with something of his aim of confiscating the identity of the man of wealth and status.[13] With Brabantio's white ewe in his keeping, has not Othello in some symbolic degree become the much-beloved in Venice?

In any event, figuring the elopement as a thievish rape of Brabantio or a form of economic cannibalism points up the undercur-

rent of primitive struggle in the contest between the Moor and the
Venetian. Civilized Venice may be the scene, but Othello and Brabantio, like the African cannibals "that each other eat," are engaged in
nothing less than a life or death struggle. Iago says as much when he
announces to the distraught father that because his daughter is gone
"[his] heart is burst" (1.1.88). Or if it has not burst already, it soon
will: when the marriage is confirmed and Brabantio is declared the
loser, Iago's metaphors are unmetaphored—Brabantio dies. "Poor
Desdemon!" Gratiano says, addressing her dead body, "I am glad thy
father's dead. / Thy match was mortal to him" (5.2.211).

Property is status, and status is life. When Brabantio enters
the Senate crying "My daughter! O, my daughter!" it is difficult not to
hear echoes of another Venetian property-owner similarly robbed,
who cried "My daughter! O my ducats! O my daughter! / Fled with a
Christian!" (*Merchant*, 2.8). Brabantio's refrain is just the reverse—
"Fled with a barbarian!"—but the effect is the same. "Dead?" the
Duke exclaims, and Brabantio answers "Ay, to me" (1.3.61). Better
dead or never born than so ignominiously lost (1.3.194).[14]

But of course Brabantio grieves also because his paternal love
has been betrayed; for daughters are a kind of property that is stowed
close to the heart. Hence, despite his patriarchal tirades, he takes on a
kind of minor tragic status when he joins the lovers' hands and says

> I here do give thee that with all my heart
> Which, but thou hast already, with all my heart
> I would keep from thee.   (1.3.196)

Desdemona has indeed been half his soul and much of his heart. Her
love, respect, and obedience endowed him with the life he loses when
she makes her lethal match. If Othello were not so flushed with his
victory, these facts might give him pause.

This line of interpretation suggests why Shakespeare is silent
on the question of whether Othello made an effort to secure Brabantio's approval of a conventional wedding, and it also suggests why he
has Othello welcome being found in the streets by the irate father and
brought to trial before the Senate. For a paternally approved wedding
would be collaborative, not competitive. Brabantio would give Desdemona away, rather than have her taken from him. He would not be
a loser and, more important, Othello would not be a winner. Even
being a winner is not enough; you must be a proclaimed winner. A
private marriage, though it may confirm Othello's victory, is insuffi-

ciently conspicuous. For part of the point of possessing property is to publicize your value.

Thus the virtue of the trial is twofold: by proclaiming Brabantio's resistance to the marriage it increases Desdemona's value as a prize, and it publicly confirms Othello's victory over both the rival father and his previously marriage-resistant daughter. Even the Duke speaks to Brabantio as to a vanquished warrior:

> Good Brabantio,
> Take up this mangled matter at the best.
> Men do their broken weapons rather use
> Than their bare hands.   (1.3.174)

But Brabantio cannot defend himself with broken weapons, and so he dies. Othello also risks death, by venturing his life on Desdemona's testimony (1.3.120). But he survives. Like the warrior who challenges death in battle and wins, he acquires the symbolic immortality that Brabantio loses.[15] He who wins Desdemona wins life and greater being.

Of course Desdemona shares in this uplifting movement. By affirming that she went with Othello freely, she redefines her own status. In fact when Brabantio declares that her example would teach him to "hang clogs" on his other children, if he had any, the situation apparently reverses itself. Becoming Othello's wife has freed her from being tethered, however loosely, as Brabantio's daughterly chattel. Moreover, the marriage is itself sublimated, since when Desdemona asks to accompany Othello to Cyprus so that "the rites for why [she] loves] him" may be enacted (1.3.260), his reply makes it clear that love, not lust, rules in his heart. For he "begs it" too, "not to please the palate of [his] appetite. . . . But to be free and bounteous to her mind." Such nobility seems to give credence to Desdemona's percipience:

> My heart's subdued
> Even to the utmost pleasure of my lord.
> I saw Othello's visage in his mind,
> And to his honors and his valiant parts
> Did I my soul and fortunes consecrate.   (254)

But Freudian and Venetian civilization comes at the cost of various discontents. Sex, given Othello's puritanical speech about its "young affects" being "defunct" or at least moderated in him by age and reason (1.3.266), is not one of them. His later violence is not the product of repressed sexual desire, as I shall argue further on. For the moment, however, the discontent of note has more to do with property than with sex. Othello is not a thief, nor is Desdemona stolen goods. He does not simply possess her, he owns her outright, legally. Yet this is not altogether reassuring. Monogamy is no doubt an improvement on abduction and rape; but here, in its economic aspect, as the masculine ownership of feminine goods, it casts a shadow over the triumph of romantic love. Even romantic love must be sealed in marriage by a contract.

4. Wives, Whores, and Emilia

Late in the play Lodovico speaks of Othello as a man held to be "all in all sufficient" (4.1.266)—a phrase suggestive of stoic independence but also disconcertingly reminiscent of Richard Crookback's "I am myself alone" and of Aristotle's remark that the self-sufficient man must be either a beast or a god.[16] Self-sufficient men should not need women. But as Othello demonstrates by self-righteously assigning Desdemona to a separate ship, self-sufficient men *do* need women—in order to prove that they can do without them. When the trumpets sound, warriors like Othello are particularly anxious to set women and sex at a safe remove from their military activities. Warriors, however, are merely a conspicuous example of a common cultural practice. After all, even the unmilitaristic scholars in *Love's Labour's Lost* feel obliged to shun women in order to expend their energies in properly platonic ways. It is a commonplace in Shakespeare that men marginalize women to privilege the manly virtues and that both men and women marginalize whores to privilege the feminine virtue of chastity.

"A man's relation to his whore," according to the Puritans of Shakespeare's day, "was that of owner. Her services had been bought and he might treat her in any way which gave him pleasure." The key word here is *pleasure*, for it was the indulgence in wanton, wasted pleasure—the surplus value of laboring in the sexual mills to produce children—that characterized whoring and offended Puritans and Humanists alike.[17]

As long as sex could yield pleasure, harlotry could not be confined to whorehouses. The impeccably chaste Desdemona says "I cannot say 'whore,' / It does abhor me now I speak the word" (4.2.163), but if the word *whore* lies dormant in her speech may not whorishness itself lie dormant in her feminine nature? Not just that married sex may be as sinfully pleasurable as the wanton variety but also that wives run the same risk as their fallen sisters of becoming masculine property. As we have seen in the Senate Scene, Othello is anxious to disclaim a sexual interest in Desdemona; their love—*his* at least—is pure and undefiled. Hence when it *is* besmirched or thought to be, he treats his fallen wife like whorish property—insulting her, striking her, ultimately taking his murderous pleasure of her in bed. But Shakespeare casts Desdemona in the role of masculine property long before she is labeled a whore. Even during the Senate Scene, where her having freely chosen Othello is decisive, what is confirmed by an exclusively masculine governing body is the patriarchal system in which a woman passes from one man's keeping into another's. Desdemona chooses Othello, but the Senate chooses which man she rightly belongs to and whether or not she can accompany him to Cyprus. Her love for the Moor may platonically transcend such sublunar considerations as age, color, and nationality. She may even, in rejecting Venice's curled darlings for the Moor, be said to reject Venice itself for the Moor. And the Senate may license this freedom. But at the same time her status as a dependent in a world of masculine power is quietly affirmed.

This masculine appropriation of women in Venice helps explain why Othello's faith in Desdemona succumbs with such surprising ease to Iago's beguilements. He loses faith in part because he never really had any. Though he endows his wife with heavenly qualities, deep down he suspects, like any other husband, the sorry truth.[18] Thus Iago's insinuations issue from a kind of collective masculine unconscious into which men's anxieties about women's whorishness have been driven so that they may take uneasy comfort from illusions of feminine sublimity, addressing their wives as "my fair warrior" and "my soul's joy" (2.1.180, 182). Iago is the returner-of-the-repressed. Even Brabantio contributes to restore the cynical view: "Look to her, Moor, if thou hast eyes to see. / She has deceived her father, and may thee" (1.3.295). Not only *may* but, in hindsight, was bound to, Othello realizes:

> Yet, 'tis the plague of great ones;
> Prerogatived are they less than the base.
> 'Tis destiny unshunnable, like death.
> Even then this forked plague is fated to us
> When we do quicken. (3.3.279)

"When we do quicken"—that is, when we are born. As though that
dark and vicious place where we are got and from which we are "delivered" irremediably sullies our lives. It certainly sullies women's
lives. Not even marital ownership can manage these jades: "That we
can call these delicate creatures ours, / And not their appetites"
(3.3.275). The trouble is, they simply refuse to act like property. Or,
rather, they *do* act like property—the kind of common property that
whores constitute. And so: "Villain, be sure thou prove my love a
whore!" (3.3.365)—which is at this point tantamount to saying "Be
sure thou prove my love a woman!"

One woman, Emilia, plays an interesting role in this connection. Although a wife herself, she seems to mediate between wives
and whores, between Desdemona and Bianca.[19] At first glance she
would seem to confirm Othello's fears about the irrepressible sensuality of women that leads husbands to their horned fate. In her
conversation with Desdemona not long before the murder, she confesses, albeit ironically in an effort to cheer her mistress, all the
failings that men attribute to women (4.3). To Desdemona's query if
there "be women do abuse their husbands / In such gross kind," she
replies "There be some such, no question" (4.3.65). In fact she
herself would "do such a deed" if the price were right—if the tag
read "all the world" for instance, because "who would not make her
husband a cuckold to make him a monarch?" (70, 78–79).

Worse than that, however, Emilia demystifies the prevailing
view that this kind of sexual duplicity is virtually genetic in women. Is
such behavior wrong? she asks. "Why the wrong is but a wrong in the
world; and having the world for your labor, 'tis a wrong in your own
world, and you might quickly make it right." In other words, morality is legislated by property owners; if you own the world, as men do,
you define right as what you do and wrong as what women do, even if
both do the same thing for the same reasons:

> What is it that they do
> When they change us for others? Is it sport?
> I think it is. And doth affection breed it?
> I think it doth. Is it frailty that thus errs?
> It is so too. And have not we affections,
> Desires for sport, and frailty, as men have?
> Then let them use us well; else let them know,
> The ills we do, their ills instruct us so.

Emilia casts herself as a feminine Shylock here—"Hath not a Jew eyes?" . . . "Hath not a woman affections?" She catechizes the sexual double standard in her Venice as he does the double citizenry of Jew and Christian in his, and finds it no less arbitrary—an instrument designed to divide into a privileged *ours* and a condemned *theirs* what is indivisibly human in nature.

But Emilia's view of adultery is a half-truth that can no more be told in Venice than, say, Falstaff's debunking half-truths about honor can be told in martial England—although Shakespeare manages to tell both in the theater. Certainly Desdemona does not want to hear it, not for all the world. Desdemona does not own the world— men do; and she is content to live in and be defined by that world, at least up to a point. The definition she receives there is that of an incomplete creature, as she admitted herself when during her courtship she said "she wished / That heaven had made her such a man" (1.3.164). In accord with Aristotle's principle that "the female is passive, material, and deprived, desiring the male in order to become complete," Desdemona longs either to *be* "such a man" herself or to have one made *for* her.[20] In either case, lacking a perfected self of her own, she becomes the supplemental property first of a father, then of a husband. Her freedom to leave her father becomes merely the freedom to become (ambiguously) enthralled by Othello, which she does so willingly that his increasingly harsh treatment of her only fortifies her love. "I would you had never seen him!" Emilia says (4.3.19):

> So would not I. My love doth so approve him,
> That even his stubbornness, his checks, his frowns—
> Prithee unpin me—have grace and favor in them.

Emilia, with her worldly views about adultery, plays a role analogous to that of the Nurse in *Romeo and Juliet*. She subjects the exalted level of the action to a brief, lightly mocking critique that serves as a diversionary lightning rod, harmlessly grounding the audience's temptation to scoff at Desdemona's idealistic too-muchness.[21] For a few moments the tension relaxes as the play gathers for a climax whose tragic action will embrace Emilia the rebellious wife as ungently as it does Desdemona the obedient one.

Desdemona may honor her "Lord" as if he were a marital deity, but Emilia is less deferential to her husband Iago. When she repeats "My husband?" three times incredulously in response to

Othello's "Thy husband knew it all" (5.2.144), all the reverence conventionally accorded that title drains away. "Good gentlemen," she says,

> let me have leave to speak.
> 'Tis proper I obey [my husband], but not now.
> Perchance, Iago, I will ne'er go home. (202)

What is *proper* to a wife is that she behave like property, but obedience has its limits, and Emilia insists on speaking the truth out of love for Desdemona.

And yet in doing so she seems to cast her mistress in a lesser light, as a wife so acquiescent in her role as to become little more than a Patient Griselda whose "only defense is to maintain an appalling innocence."[22] As her husband reasserts his property rights over her and his allegiance to the male world—"Yet she must die, else she'll betray more men"! (5.2.6)—she countersigns his charter with her dying words, conferring on him the authority to dispose of his chattel as he wishes. "O who hath done this deed?" Emilia asks. "Nobody; I myself. Farewell. / Commend me to my kind lord. O, farewell"—an exoneration of Othello that brands her in his eyes "a liar gone to burning hell! / 'Twas I that killed her."

5. Beyond Property

How to interpret Desdemona's dying? A cynical view of it would argue that her self-sacrificial death is designed to reinforce patriarchal illusions by portraying selfless and surrendering love in marriage as the ultimate in feminine fulfillment. On that, after all, most of the authorities agree: philosophy, theology, medicine, law, ancient literature, the chain of Degree, an informal storehouse of commonplaces.[23] Even Christ can be called on to testify to the spiritual virtue that accrues to obediently suffering wives like Desdemona. Thus in Quarto 1 (5.2.85) Desdemona's cry "O Lord, Lord, Lord" as she is being smothered is reminiscent, as Robert G. Hunter notes, of Christ's *"Eli, Eli, lama sabacthani."*[24] In Desdemona's case, the word *Lord* ambiguously fuses God and Othello, lending an aspect of divinity to her husband. Thus her dying submission to such a husband seems an instance of Christian *agape*, and although her example is not likely to encourage other wives to suffer smothering gladly, it does authorize them to smile bravely through their tears as she dies.

This reading of the murder scene presupposes a Shakespeare who is at best an unwitting advocate of the patriarchal values of his time, as indeed some critics maintain.[25] However, one might argue just the reverse, that Shakespeare does not so much exploit as expose this sort of reading, much as Nietzsche in *The Genealogy of Morals* exposes the tactics by which Christianity pacified the oppressed by making their suffering not merely endurable but the very needle's eye to salvation. The function of Emilia, on this view, is to underscore the injustices of Renaissance marriage and the foolishness of Desdemona's obedience to its code.

However, both of these views place too much stress on the institution of marriage and too little on Desdemona and Othello. Desdemona may be a tragic instance of the victimization of women in a social order founded on masculine property rights, but she is more, and less, than that. After all, she did not pledge her troth to the institution of marriage but to Othello. Before that she had proved, Brabantio says, "So opposite to marriage that she shunned / The wealthy curled darlings of our nation," to her father's palpable dismay (1.2.68). She has refused to put herself on the marriage block and become a piece of moveable property in the monetary communications between two wealthy families. Similarly, in marrying Othello she does not submit to convention but defies it, transcending her potential status as property by freely choosing the Moor despite many daunting differences.[26]

Just as her love for Othello acquitted him of the charge of thievish witchery in Act 1, so it acquits him now, at least momentarily, of the charge of murder. However, Desdemona's dying words are not a declaration of conformity to the institution of marriage or an acknowledgment of the rights of husbands. They testify rather to the transcendent marriage of what Sonnet 116 calls a true mind, of a love that is "not Time's fool" even at this final turning point when "rosy lips and cheeks / Within his bending sickle's compass come."

Nor is Desdemona as selflessly submissive as the cynical reading implies. For before she says "Nobody; I myself" she first declares "A guiltless death I die." That is, she retains a clear enough sense of her own identity to reject the shameful death Othello tries to impose on her, as in fact she did in the Murder Scene earlier.[27] Her refusal there to play *pharmakos* to Othello's priest makes it clear that the murder Othello thought "a sacrifice" turns out to be a sacrifice after all, by being a murder. What is purged, however, is not Desdemona's sins but Othello's illusions, and beyond them, the illusions of masculine authority. For beneath those illusions is simply the threat of physical violence, a point made with surprising eloquence by Emilia when she too is threatened by Othello: "Thou hast not half that power to do me harm / As I have to be hurt" (5.2.169). Emilia's remark casts light retrospectively on the Murder Scene. For when Desdemona denies her guilt point by point, she obliges Othello to confess in murderous action that his authority over her derives not from moral or spiritual superiority, nor from personal perfection of soul or masculine completeness of human nature, but from force itself, from nothing more sacred than the power to do harm.

As Simone Weil observed, force, however sophisticated, rests in the final analysis on the capacity to transform a human into a corpse.[28] The threat of that force registers quietly in Desdemona's talk, as she prepares for bed, about the maid "called Barbary" whose love forsook her (4.3.28). For of course *Barbary* echoes Iago's jibe about Brabantio's "daughter [being] covered with a Barbary horse" (1.1.112), which in turn calls up images of a marriage consummated at the Sagittary under the sign of the centaur. During the Murder Scene the centaur aptly represents the division in Othello between the humane love that cherishes and the barbaric force that rapes and kills. Ultimately Brabantio's daughter *is* barbarously "covered," not by a snorting centaur but by a proprietary husband claiming absolute title to his wife's body.

Having exposed this truth about masculine property rights, Desdemona delivers her final speech in which she willingly submits—not to force, but to Othello. When she absolves him with the words "Nobody; I myself. . . . Commend me to my kind lord," she announces in effect that her acceptance of his authority has derived not from his institutional status as her husband, nor from his masculine capacity to do her harm, but from consent freely given, from nothing more forceful than the "downright violence" of her own love as she declared it before the Senate: "My heart's subdued / Even to the utmost pleasure of my lord."[29]

So her sins were, as she confessed, the "loves I bear to you" (5.2.42). In this light, her dying claim to have killed herself is not entirely the lie it literally appears to be. If she did not actually kill herself, she unwittingly invited death through the nobility of a love that platonically (and foolishly) refused to register Othello's metamorphosis. Had the love she bore him been less unfailingly true, more prudently prepared to alter when it alteration found, she might well have lived. Absolute constancy has small survival value; it sins against its possessor. In these last words of hers the sin of love reasserts itself by issuing a true lie. For Desdemona's "truth" is not the scrupulously just correspondence of word to fact but the merciful "troth" of a love so deeply plighted that it bears it out beyond all bounds of property and possession.

III

Appalling Property

1. Mutual Flames

If property depends on the drawing and maintenance of property lines, then love violates property as much as theft does—and a lot more confusingly. Love, in fact, appalls property—if we steal Shakespeare's phrase from "The Phoenix and the Turtle." In that enigmatic requiem for lost love, we learn that through the dissolving action of the dead birds' mutual flame,

> Property was thus appalled
> That the self was not the same:
> Single nature's double name
> Neither two nor one was called. (37–40)

In this context property refers of course not to lands and carriages but to distinctive identity, the haecceity or quiddity that divides person from person and that ought to divide even lover from lover—but does not. And yet does. Love's fusion of distincts makes it a mystery to the intellect:

> Reason, in itself confounded,
> Saw division grow together,
> To themselves yet either neither;
> Simple were so well compounded
>
> That it cried "How true a twain
> Seemeth this concordant one!
> Love hath reason, Reason none,
> If what parts can so remain."

In Shakespeare, reason is always confounded by love's mysterious crossing of property lines.[1] Brabantio's bafflement that his daughter has compounded with the alien Moor is not essentially different from that of the lovers in *A Midsummer Night's Dream* when they find their own hearts' affections spinning like tops. Love's web is woven with magic, stewed in strange potions, bound by spells, and wantonly called forth by minor divinities and fairies. How else explain it? When Chaucer's Criseyda murmurs "Who yaf me drynke?" on seeing Troilus, she speaks for hosts of lovers wonder-struck by youth's great fancy. The uncomfortable fact is that love is a form of mutual possession, however benign. The spirits of lovers appall one another's property as those of demons do when they inexplicably take up residence in the innocent. Demonic possession is to love as a Black Mass is to the Communion. Thus it is inauspicious indeed that we have a demon as well as a true twain in *Othello*.

Unlike demons, however, love is often self-exorcising. The incantations of time—weeks, months, or years—will expel the invading spirit, leaving the miraculously concordant one a ruefully discordant two again. So it goes in the sonnets, where long hot summers make even love's lilies fester worse than weeds. For that matter, the phoenix and the turtle are dead and, with that paradigm lost, love is doomed to come and go with the moon.[2] It does not augur well for love in Venice.

Still, the love of Othello and Desdemona appears to appall property in the mutual flame sense, by crossing or dissolving the well-defined borders between youth and age, white and black, citizen and stranger. It certainly appalls property, if by *property* we mean "propriety" or, more particularly, Brabantio, the propertied magnifico. Brabantio would have disposed of his daughterly property more wisely, in keeping with the institution of the fixed marriage. Despite the introduction of the companionate marriage during the Reformation, Lawrence Stone amply documents the fact that in Shakespeare's time children, and especially daughters, were "bartered like cattle" by ambitious parents who demanded and received bovine obedience from their children.[3] (It's unlikely that Brabantio intended bartering Desdemona like this, else she would already be lowing at the heels of some wealthy Venetian darling; but he does say that if he had another child "thy escape would teach me tyranny, / To hang clogs on them" [1.3.200–201].)[4] But of course the marriage of Othello and Desdemona is not of this sort. For them, patriarchal authority yields to the dominion of love, and the conquest is ratified in the Senate. Let us then take a closer look at the ways in which love appalls property, both visually and verbally.

2. Mirrors and Shifters

Desdemona has no doubt about Othello's identity; no charms have blinded her to his blackness or his age:

> I saw Othello's visage in his mind,
> And to his honors and his valiant parts
> Did I my soul and fortunes consecrate.   (1.3.253)

To see visages in minds you must look through bodies—a talent usually reserved for licensed platonists. For the rest of us, seeing is insensible to the withinness of things; it stops at the surface. Hearing, on the other hand, acknowledges interiors; it places a stethoscope to the world's chest to discover that within which passeth show. Desdemona did not see Othello's visage in his mind, she heard it. In his account of it, finding occasion to hear his stories, she "devoured up [his] discourse" and issued up a world of sighs—

> She wished she had not heard it, yet she wished
> That heaven had made her such a man. She thanked me,
> And bade me, if I had a friend that loved her,
> I should but teach him how to tell my story,
> And that would woo her. Upon this hint I spake.
> She loved me for the dangers I had passed,
> And I loved her that she did pity them.
> This only is the witchcraft I have used.   (1.3.164)

From this it seems Desdemona loved Othello not only for the dangers he had passed but especially for the words he passed on about those dangers. Even though she is speaking coyly, her claim that such a story in the mouth of a friend would successfully woo her gives a disconcerting priority to the story over its speaker. Othello's words may not be crafted by witches, but they cast a powerful spell.

Othello's remark "She loved me for the dangers I had passed, / And I loved her that she did pity them" is a mote in the eye of anyone anxious to regard the Moor as a phoenix to Desdemona's turtle. It's not that "Othello loves not Desdemona but his image of her"; rather he loves her image of him.[5] If she sees his visage in his mind, he sees in her mind not her visage but his own. Thus later on, lamenting what he now takes to be his loss, he says

> But there where I have garnered up my heart,
> Where either I must live or bear no life,

The fountain from the which my current runs
Or else dries up—to be discarded thence!   (4.2.57)

As Graham Bradshaw observes, Othello "first endows, or invests, Desdemona with unique significance, garnering up his heart by making her his storehouse of value; and then he sees her as the fountain or source, from which his life *derives* significance and value."[6]

The selflessness of love seems confused somewhat with the acquisition of property in which the owner's parts and perfect soul will be manifested rightly. From one perspective, Desdemona becomes a sublime lens through which Venice sees the true Moor. From another, she serves as a glass in which Othello sees an enhanced image of himself. Ulysses' speech to Achilles in *Troilus and Cressida* explains the optics of the matter (3.3.95):

> A strange fellow here
> Writes me that man, how clearly ever parted,
> How much in having, or without or in,
> Cannot make boast to have that which he hath,
> Nor feels not what he owes, but by reflection;
> As when his virtues, aiming upon others,
> Heat them, and they retort that heat again
> To the first giver.

Achilles replies:

> This is not strange, Ulysses.
> The beauty that is borne here in the face
> The bearer knows not, but commends itself
> To others' eyes; nor doth the eye itself,
> That most pure spirit of sense, behold itself,
> Not going from itself, but eye to eye opposed
> Salutes each other with each other's form.
> For speculation turns not to itself
> Till it hath traveled and is mirrored there
> Where it may see itself. This is not strange at all.

Ulysses agrees but adds that his writer

> expressly proves
> That no man is the lord of anything,
> Though in and of him there be much consisting,
> Till he communicate his parts to others;

> Nor doth he of himself know them for aught
> Till he behold them formed in the applause
> Where th' are extended . . .

Perhaps Ulysses' unidentified correspondent was an ancestor of Hegel, who later wrote: "Self-consciousness exists in and for itself when, and by the fact that, it so exists for another; that is, it exists only in being acknowledged."[7] Othello is a case in point. For the Moor's belief that he is the lord and owner of his most valuable parts is confirmed by the applause of Desdemona, whom he therefore loves. Freud's views on the formation of self are also surprisingly relevant to Othello's courtship. He observes that we have at bottom two sexual objects: ourselves and the woman who cares for us (in both senses). Narcissistically we want to identify lovingly with an object (usually the mother) whose love for us reflects and enhances our self-love, and at the same time we want (in what he calls the "anaclitic object-choice") to possess another object (usually also the mother). In the present case Desdemona satisfies both desires.[8]

Or we could note a resemblance here to Jacques Lacan's famous "mirror stage," that crucial first phase in the shaping of a sense of self, in which the child whose body is still uncoordinated sees itself reflected as a unified whole by the mirror.[9] Not that Othello is a child, but he is a borderer or a threshold character, a man of uncertain status still fashioning an identity for himself in Venice. For of course the process by which we shape fictions about the *I* extends well beyond childhood, fairly literally in some cases, as Rembrandt's one hundred or so self-portraits employing mirrors attest, but more often metaphorically, as Stephen J. Greenblatt's studies in Renaissance self-fashioning indicate.[10]

Even a literal mirror is a kind of metaphor inasmuch as its glassy image presents an illusion of identity; it is and is not the child, just as the reflecting Other in Ulysses' speech is and is not the man who owns and does not own himself. Desdemona stands in a similar relation to Othello; she is an external metaphor that reflects his inner parts. That is true whether we regard her as Othello's representative property or as his metaphorizing mirror. The fact that these two modes of reflection are both applicable underscores Othello's peculiar need to be manifested rightly.[11] For as it is, his black appearance betrays him; even Desdemona must look through his corporeal surface to value his mind. His blackness is a lying metaphor, a superficial analog to a mysteriously perfect self inside. This produces a kind of chain of metaphoric signification, working from inside out: Othello's perfect soul is metaphorically substituted for (and misrepresented) by his skin, which is in turn metaphorically substituted for by Desdemona, who manifests him rightly. When Desdemona is called to testify, her words scrub away the blackness that obscured Othello's inner virtues, causing the Duke to say to Brabantio, "Your son-in-law is far more fair than black" (1.3.293).

Calling Desdemona's mirrorings of Othello "metaphors" lends them a verbal dimension that suggests an extension of Lacan's mirror stage. The mirror stage constitutes the gateway between the *imaginary* and the *symbolic*. The child begins to acquire a sense of its body via the mirror, but its final sense of self will take place within language. Thus, in social scientese, a three-phase process of "identity-acquisition" would feature mirrors, proper names, and shifters.[12] On this view, as the child's amorphous body coalesces into a distinct whole within the mirror, so its nebulous sense of personal identity coalesces and takes shape at a later point within its name. The proper name improves on the mirror not only because it reflects the whole child, instead of merely its bodily surfaces, but also because it has a proprietary self-reference lacking in the mirror. A mirror, after all, reflects my image when I am in front of it, but it is equally hospitable to your image when you are in front of it, whereas my proper name refers to me alone, no matter who says it.[13] In the fixed singularity of my name I sense my own stability, and in its repeatability I register my own constancy through time.

The kind of security offered by my proper name stands me in good stead when I come to learn the use of shifters.[14] For shifters (deictics, *embrayeurs*) are particularly hard to grasp because they have no reference independent of the context in which they are spoken. Somewhat like the hospitable mirror, *I* in my voice means me, but in your voice it means you. Similarly, the reference of *left* and *right*, *here* and *there*, *yesterday*, and *at that time* depends on the scene of discourse and who is speaking. Thus to understand *left* and *right*, say, children must be able to put themselves in another's place; and to understand *I*, *me*, and *mine* they must be willing to share pronouns that seem their own personal property. In other words, to use shifters I must become a social animal, whereas to answer to my proper name I need merely recognize my individual discreteness from others. The price of my using *I* properly is to yield to others (when they speak it) the private and unique interiority from which that pronoun seems so naturally to issue from *my* lips, mouth, throat, self, soul; and the price of my using *you* and *he* properly is to yield to others the right to speak of me as an object.

This gets me around to suggesting that the verbal equivalent to the spiritual love of the phoenix and the turtle is the reciprocal interchange of personal pronouns in the murmurings of lovers. Thus Romeo and Juliet discard the fixed names that define their (antagonistic) public identities as Montague and Capulet in favor of the social intimacy of *I* and *thou* in the garden. This abandonment of family names for personal pronouns would surely offend their propertied parents; and it does appall property itself, since as a reflection of the mutuality of their love *I* is now Romeo but also Juliet yet also neither one nor the other, as the phoenix and the turtle were "To themselves yet either neither."

Love in Venice, however, is not the same as love in Verona. Shifters there do not shift as readily, nor are they shared so generously. In the specular image of Desdemona, Othello sees an aggrandized version of his own *I* that, unfortunately, somewhat eclipses her own title to selfhood. Shakespeare makes the point in several ways— first, by narrating instead of dramatizing their love. Narration inevitably entails an *I-me/she-her* relationship: "*She* loved *me* for the dangers *I* had passed, / And *I* loved *her* that *she* did pity them." By its nature, Othello's narrative robs Desdemona of an *I*, even when her speech is recorded:

> *She* thanked me,
> And bade me, if I had a friend that loved *her*,
> I should but teach him how to tell my story,
> And that would woo *her*. Upon this hint I spake.

Othello's entire speech to the Senate is self-possessive. The words to the Senate are his, the words to Brabantio and Desdemona were his, the past he told them about was his, and as a result Desdemona is his. He speaks proprietarily of "*my* redemption," "*my* travels," "*my* discourse," "*my* youth," and so on. And as he possesses the possessive *my*, so he possesses the subjective *I*. Othello is *I*, *I* is Othello. He is not only a capitalist of self but a self-capitalizer.

However, much of this egocentricity comes with the narrative territory. Whoever tells a story gets to be, not *it*, but *I*. Even when Vergil shifts into dialogue, with characters assuming *I-thou* relationships, it is his ventriloquistic voice we hear singing "of arms and the man." In the narrative mode only the narrator speaks; everyone else is merely quoted. Thus narrative converts the shifter *I* into something approximating a proper name. As long as the Moor is telling his stories, *I* refers as exclusively to him as *Othello* does. In drama, on the other hand, no one has exclusive possession of the *I* because in it, as in no other mode, characters truly speak in their own voices. Had Shakespeare chosen to dramatize Othello's courtship, he would have been obliged to give Desdemona a voice of her own. But that is the point: Shakespeare is not in the giving mood. Kept off stage as long as possible, Desdemona remains merely the spoken-of.

Even when Desdemona finally does come on stage to speak in her own voice, she and Othello are not granted a moment of privacy, largely, to be sure, owing to the public nature of the occasion. Nevertheless, in the first act Desdemona never uses the word *I* in addressing Othello; and although he calls her *thee* on one occasion, elsewhere she is without exception a third-person *she*.[15] As a result, although Desdemona is the focus of desire in Venice, it is she even more than Othello who seems the outsider in this first act.

This suggests that property is only partly appalled in *Othello*. The Moor takes possession of Desdemona, who willingly yields her proper self. He is he, and she is he, but she is not fully she as an I, or they are not fully they as a we. In any event Desdemona remains to some extent the prize of property for which Othello and Brabantio (and in the background, Roderigo) have contested. Like all good Elizabethan women, she is supposed to fulfill her femininity in marriage and child-bearing, but like them too she is not allowed a full identity either before or after marriage. She remains on the periphery of a masculine world, an escapee from paternal restraint, granted the crucial word at the trial, accorded value, yet condemned either to remain the property of her father or to become the property of her husband. Thus although the comedic structure of the first act endorses the mutuality of love, Desdemona's status as property and her consequent exclusion from the pronominal community of *I* and *thou* augurs ominously for her future. Indeed her reduction to a *she* that at times verges on *it* may be said to forecast her ultimate alienation and death.

3. Looking and Listening

That the Moor's love is flawed from the beginning in ways that predict its ultimate shattering is also suggested if we consider it from a sensory perspective. Actually, as *perspective* implies, I have already been preoccupied with the visual aspects of love, and especially with the mirroring manner in which Othello reinforces his sense of self by making his outward property reflective of his inner properties in accord with Ulysses' speech about the eye's goings and comings. That speech perfectly illustrates the privileging of the eye in Western epistemology.[16] To know is to see and vice versa, which means that our knowledge is primarily oriented to the "out-there"—to the nature we see directly or to the charts, books, and instruments that bring it into intellectual focus. The "in-here" is more difficult. To know our insides we must project ourselves outward somehow to become visible—in thermometers, X-rays, or, less precisely, property. The difficulty of course is that we cannot externalize ourselves fully; we cannot be converted into objects. To make others into property, as Othello does to some extent with Desdemona, is to objectify them; but people stubbornly retain their subjectivity, as he suggests when he complains to Iago "that we can call these delicate creatures ours, / And not their appetites" (3.3.275).

Despite Western philosophy, then, Othello cannot know Desdemona by looking at her. For sight reflects surfaces, and appetites lie within, situated according to Renaissance psychology in the liver. Livers that lust, hearts that love, souls that long for eternity are all part of the mysterious within. If seeing is knowing, then to know about livers, hearts, and souls we must, as surgeons so ominously put it, go in and take a look. Unfortunately, the price of this kind of knowledge is often death. As Wordsworth pointed out, we murder to dissect. Even without going in, however, sight-knowledge involves a kind of murder, because a perception of surfaces necessarily transforms a human into an object by killing off the very interiority that makes him or her distinctively human. Most important, it kills off speech, the continuum of expressive sound that melds the human within and the world without.[17]

Because it is keyed to surfaces, sight is Othello's enemy in Venice, where the color of virtue is not black but white. Perhaps for that very reason he is himself preoccupied with Desdemona's surface appearance. Her external beauty, insofar as she is his property and reflects his virtues, will close the gap between his inwardly "perfect soul" and his outwardly imperfect surface. When he greets her on Cyprus it is the sight of her that produces his "O my fair warrior!" (2.1.180). Later he is annoyed by her speeches on behalf of Cassio, yet as he watches her depart he cries "Excellent wretch! Perdition catch my soul / But I do love thee!" (3.3.92). A bit further on, shaken by Iago's insinuations, he demands "ocular proof" of her infidelity (3.3.366); insists with increasing fury upon seeing the handkerchief ("Fetch it, let me see it" [3.4.87]); obtains his ocular proof in Iago's suggestive stagings ("Did you perceive how he laughed at his vice?" . . . "And did you see the handkerchief?" [4.1.170, 172]); and sets about devising an appropriate death.

Desdemona's death is predicted in both senses: sight and sound. The one thing worse than being looked upon as an object is not being looked upon at all. If looking *at* someone tends to deny the other's humanity, refusing to look at all denies the other's existence. When Othello strikes Desdemona (4.1.240) he reduces her to a bodily object, but when he banishes her from his sight—"Get you away . . . Hence, avaunt!" (259, 261)—he annihilates her.

Yet her surface remains diabolically lovely. In a vicious parallel to Desdemona's seeing through Othello's outer blackness to his inner virtues—"I saw Othello's visage in his mind"—Othello now sees through her fairness to a supposed blackness within. Offended by such doubleness, as a good platonist would be, he would have what lies within rise and fuse with the surface, much as he sought to exteriorize his inner virtues in Desdemona herself. To bring about this unity now, he would grant her a voice, but only if her words will paint her inward sins upon her outward form:

> Come, swear it, damn thyself,
> Lest, being like one of heaven, the devils themselves
> Should fear to seize thee. (4.2.35)

But Desdemona perversely refuses to confess, so that in the Brothel Scene Othello is baffled by the (un)apparent contrast between her outward looks and her inward villainy, she whose "well-painted passion" of tearful distress conceals her errant heart (4.1.258), who is "so lovely fair" and yet as polluted as summer flies in a shambles (4.2.66), who looks like an angel but lusts like a whore.

Perhaps the most telling of Othello's likenings occurs when he asks "Was this fair paper, this most goodly book, / Made to write 'whore' upon?" (4.2.71). Whether blazoned with the word *whore* or even fairer phrasings, Desdemona is reduced entirely to a two-dimensional surface on whom others make their impress. The significance of this is suggested by comparison to the whorish Cressida, of whom

Ulysses says "There's language in her eye, her cheek, her lip, / Nay, her foot speaks" (4.5.55). Cressida is a corrupted body too, but she is not all body; her body is simply a seductive medium through which she expresses herself. Hence the metaphors of speech. But Desdemona is not granted speech; she is a page, and not a page where she writes her feelings but where she is written upon by the "pens" of other men.[18]

Yet when Othello comes to kill her, he cannot help wanting to preserve "that whiter skin of hers than snow / And smooth as monumental alabaster."[19] After all, it was in that statuesque white mirror that he once saw himself so favorably reflected. And so instead of stabbing her or tearing her all to pieces, as he had furiously vowed to do, he smothers her, employing a mode of murder that preserves her appearance while stopping her speech—"But while I say one prayer," she begs, but Othello will hear no more prayers.

To digress for a moment, I might observe that Desdemona's request to pray calls to mind the element of faith involved in listening to speech as opposed to seeing. Seeing requires little in the way of faith because what is seen is visibly present, whereas speech is symbolic and belated, referring to what is absent and in the past. When Bacon lost faith in the verbal honesty of the old-time scholastics, he stopped listening to Aquinas and began scrutinizing nature for the truth.[20] Othello, having lost faith in Desdemona's honesty, subjects her truth to a kind of mock-Baconian experiment in which he sees precisely what Iago wants him to see and transforms what he sees into certain knowledge. Once he has locked his certainty in place, none of his senses carries conviction. In the Murder Scene Desdemona's attractions—visual ("that whiter skin of hers than snow"), olfactory ("I'll smell thee on the tree"), tactile ("One more [kiss], one more"), and gustatory ("So sweet was ne'er so fatal")—combine to appeal her case against the mind's foregone conclusions, but can no more obtain a fair "hearing" than her words. When his own speech grows frantic, he lets his hands speak for him.

Desdemona does not die immediately. When Emilia comes to the door crying "My lord, my lord! What, ho! My lord, my lord!" the distracted Othello, unsure whether he hears Emilia or Desdemona herself, mutters "What voice is this? Not dead? Not yet quite dead?" and kills her a second time. In view of his increasing tendency to tar Desdemona with the brush of universal feminine corruption, it is fitting that he should be momentarily unable to distinguish her voice from that of Emilia. Fitting too that although Emilia briefly experiences the same uncertainty when Desdemona actually does speak ("O, lord, what cry is that?" [122]) she quickly recognizes her ("Out, and alas, that was my lady's voice") and begs her to speak further.

Thus in the killing of Desdemona Shakespeare takes to murderous extremes the implications of the old saying that children and women and other social inferiors should be seen and not heard.[21] For to deny speech to people is to deprive them of one important way in which they can reveal the interiority that makes them human. For Shakespeare, as for his contemporaries, speech is the distinctively human gift. "Language," according to Ben Jonson, "most shewes a man: speake that I may see thee. It springs out of the most retired, and inmost parts of us, and is the Image of the Parent of it, the mind. No glasse renders a mans forme, or likenesse, so true as his speech."[22] Repeatedly in Shakespeare the test of life itself is not whether a character can be seen but whether he or she can be heard. "If she pertain to life, let her speak too," Leontes says of the statuesque Hermione (5.3.113), and the Ghost can tramp back and forth as much as it likes in *Hamlet*, but Horatio keeps crying "Speak to me!" to verify its reality (1.1.128–39). If the sign of life is speech, the sign of death is silence. Othello's reliance on ocular proof entails an increasing refusal to hear Desdemona speak. Which means that she is reduced to a silence tantamount to death even before he kills her.

At the end of the play, Desdemona speaks only faintly for herself—"A guiltless death I die"—while maintaining silence as regards Othello—"Nobody; I myself" (5.2.127, 129). Her selflessness is measured by Emilia's rebellious insistence on speaking (227):

No, I will speak as liberal as the north.
Let heaven and men and devils, let them all,
All, all, cry shame against me, yet I'll speak.

Of course the cost to Emilia of telling the truth, of liberating herself as a person from her subservience as wife, is death—as it was also for her mistress, insofar as Desdemona's disobedient insistence on her innocence maddened the priestly Othello and hastened her death.

When Othello discovers what he has done, he turns to the dead Desdemona and says,

Now, how dost thou look now? O ill-starred wench!
Pale as thy smock! When we shall meet at compt,
This look of thine will hurl my soul from heaven,
And fiends will snatch at it. (5.2.281)

Even dead, she remains a "heavenly sight" (287). At the very least, she still looks alive, especially on stage where in the boy who plays her she still *is* alive. The only difference is that she is "still" in the double sense of being motionless and silent. Of the two, silence is the more deadly stillness: you can see corpses, you cannot hear them, as you can see humans without registering their humanity until they speak, and sometimes even after.

Desdemona's own humanity was most publicly evident in the Senate Scene when she was called on to provide the definitive testimony in behalf of Othello. Then everyone listened to her voice, attended to her feelings, and took her word. What came from within her gave the lie to surface appearances and converted her from a stolen object into a consenting woman. Even such a moment, however, was slightly shadowed by the fact that she had been sent for less to speak of herself than to speak of Othello. "Send for the lady to the Saggitary," he had offered, "And let her speak of me before her father" (1.3.118). Othello will listen avidly when the subject of her discourse is himself. He will even stake his life on her report, on the image of himself reflected in her speech. Later, however, when she speaks not of him but of Cassio, he loses interest quickly; and when she speaks of herself in and before the Murder Scene he will not listen at all. "It is too late." In a sense it was always too late. Thus in death she remains a lovely object but a silent one, devoid of an interior that was never fully conferred upon her to begin with.

4. He That Was Othello

Proper names, as discussed earlier, play a significant role in fixing a sense of identity. Thus it is not surprising that the unfixing of Othello's identity should be accompanied by a distancing of his proper name, as when he says, late in the play, "That's he that was Othello. Here I am."[23] This unnaming of the self was hinted at when he concluded his famous farewell speech by announcing that "Othello's occupation's gone" (3.3.362), and was confirmed in the Brothel Scene when he said,

> I cry you mercy, then.
> I took you for that cunning whore of Venice
> That married with Othello.   (4.2.88)

On these two occasions Othello speaks his own name for the first time in the play—"speaks" but hardly proclaims. It's one thing to announce "This is I, Hamlet, the Dane!" but quite another to use one's name as if it were a third-person pronoun: "That's he that was Othello." As though the purity of the name itself were besmirched, Othello packs up an *I* and self-protectively vacates the nominal premises of *Othello*. It is *I* who call you a cunning whore, but the man you made ridiculous was someone called *Othello*.

At the opening of the Murder Scene, however, the Moor seems sufficiently recovered to answer Desdemona's "Who's there? Othello?" by saying "Ay, Desdemona." But *Othello* is now an uncomfortable role he is trying to play, a once natural identity he reasserts but can keep intact only momentarily before the old rage is upon him. Then he is forced to call what he intended to do a murder instead of a sacrifice, and to call himself a stony-hearted killer instead of a priestly purger.

When he next refers to himself as *Othello* Desdemona is dead, and he is a murderer under arrest. Seizing a sword, he briefly threatens violence and then gives it up:

> Do you go back dismayed? 'Tis a lost fear;
> Man but a rush against Othello's breast,
> And he retires. Where should Othello go?

By reverting to the third-person proper name here, he again measures his shame by the distance he puts between himself and his identity. This leads within a few lines to the explicit division of self of "That's he that was Othello. Here I am." By now, even the common *I*, which entertains rakish visitors as hospitably as a whore, is preferable to *Othello*. Thus at the end, when he says "Speak of me as I am," who knows who or what this *I* stands for? In his own phrase he is both an objective *me* and a subjective *I*, and on the verge of becoming a third-person pronoun in the story to be told back in Venice of—

> *one* that loved not wisely but too well;
> Of *one* not easily jealous, but, being wrought,
> Perplexed in the extreme; of *one* whose hand,
> Like the base Indian, threw a pearl away
> Richer than all *his* tribe; of *one* whose subdued eyes,
> Albeit unused to the melting mood,
> Drops tears as fast as the Arabian trees
> Their medicinable gum. . . .

The pathos of his dying moment lies in his finally addressing Desdemona in the language of *I* and *thou* at a time when these two shifters have become as immobile as she:

> I kissed thee ere I killed thee. No way but this,
> Killing myself, to die upon a kiss.

This is a sad parody both of the sexual act and of the fusion of identities in the selfless exchange of *I* and *thou* in the speech of love. Othello's repetition of *thee* marks this as perhaps his most loving moment. Yet an affirmation of Desdemona's selfhood comes ironically late, at a time when he must cast her in the accusative case, not as a *thou* to say and do, but as a *thee* to be done unto, as indeed she has been throughout the play.

As that *thee* underscores, Othello is now, as in a sense he always was, in sole possession of the *I*—one second before his grammatical conversion into a permanent *he:*

> This did *I* fear, but thought *he* had no weapon;
> For *he* was great of heart.

That is Cassio speaking. Having been suspected of taking Othello's place in bed, having officially taken his place as governor of Cyprus, and now about to "seize upon the fortunes of the Moor, / For they succeed on [him]," it is appropriate that he appropriate what Othello mistakenly regarded as his most private property of all, the first-person pronoun.

Signs, Speech, and Self

1. Signs and Ensigns

Earlier I suggested that Othello solves his semiotic dilemma—how to manifest his perfect soul publicly when its most apparent outward sign is his devilishly black skin and moorish looks—by acquiring marital property, by projecting his virtues outward into Venice through the refracting prism of Desdemona's beauty. But marital property is merely one of several modes of expression in this play, and in the present chapter I want to explore more fully how Othello's self seeks signs of various sorts in which to publicize its identity.

As Desdemona's case indicates, the most natural or at least most apparent sign of inner meaning is the body. The lovely Desdemona is a perfect example of Pietro Bembo's neoplatonic contention in *The Book of the Courtier* that the body is on the whole an accurate index of inner virtue and that beauty in particular is a circle whose center is goodness.[1] Shakespeare, however, entertains neoplatonism only when it suits him. Lacking the courtier's implicit faith in signs, he founds his play on the rupture between outward signifiers and inward signifieds, between the Moor's evil-seeming black face and his "perfect soul," between his ancient's honest-seeming white exterior and the ulcerous evil that breeds around his heart. The body is a capricious sign; it may or may not tell the truth. But what else can you rely on? Except in the case of angels, souls do not converse with other souls directly; and most sublunar creatures lack Falstaff's instinctive ability to discern the true Prince even through buckram ("By the Lord, I knew ye as well as he that made ye!"). As Bembo himself says:

> For, finding itself deep in an earthly prison, and deprived of spiritual contemplation in exercising its office of governing the body, the soul of itself cannot clearly perceive the truth; wherefore, in order to have

knowledge, it is obliged to turn to the senses as to its source of knowledge; and so it believes them and bows before them and lets itself be guided by them, especially when [as in the young and passionate] they have so much vigor that they almost force it; and, being fallacious, they fill it with errors and false opinions.[2]

As the bodily senses are the avenue to knowing others, so, reversely, one's own body is the avenue to being known. Misrepresented by his body, however, Othello is obliged to take as the sign of his soul another body, Desdemona's. For a military man, it is like choosing a champion and staking the entire battle on single combat outside one's citadel. The analogy has a certain appropriateness here inasmuch as the semiotics of the self has a military dimension to it. Iago points it out. In Act 1, Scene 1 he tells Roderigo that with the Cypriot wars afoot he must go seek out the General:

> Though I do hate him as I do hell-pains,
> Yet, for necessity of present life,
> I must show out a flag and sign of love,
> Which is indeed but sign. (156)

Iago's interest in flag-waving here follows from his mention of the wars and derives from the fact that he is Othello's ancient, or ensign. In Elizabethan armies, "the ensign had no command or administrative function. His job was simply to carry the colors (in the middle of his band in a set battle, at the head of his band during a charge or assault) and to conduct himself in such a way as to bring honor to his person."[3] As Othello's flag-carrying ensign, then, Iago literally holds Othello's identity—or at any rate the sign of Othello's identity—in his own hands.[4] How appropriate, therefore, that he remain the Moor's ancient at the beginning of the play instead of graduating to lieutenant. For *lieutenant*, in its French sense of "in lieu of," is obviously more suitable to the Cassio whom Othello suspects of wearing his nightcap and who ultimately takes his place as commander of Cyprus.[5]

He who threads his identity into a flag, and entrusts that flag to an ensign like Iago, is in grave danger of coming apart at the seams. Externalizing one's inner meanings is hazardous even in the best of cases, even when one's flag is Desdemona. For she too is Othello's ensign in Venice, the beautiful white flag that parades the virtues and value of the Moor. To make the parallel with Iago more exact, Desdemona is not only Othello's flag but his flag-bearer as well. In this role she carries onto the sexual battlefield the handkerchief in whose magic web his identity as husband is so closely woven. When she lets that flag fall—the ultimate sin for an ensign—it passes into the keeping of Bianca, is captured as it were by that mortal enemy of all virtuous wives, the whore. At crucial points like this in *Othello*, signs take on literal significance. With the flag that betokens a chaste marriage in the possession of Bianca, Desdemona's and Othello's identities are both forfeited. In Othello's embittered imagination, she becomes a strumpet, he a purchaser of her sexual favors, and their bedroom a brothel.

We never see Iago carrying Othello's flag into battle. Instead of a sign he bears the sign of a sign—the title of ensign or ancient. Thus Desdemona's loss of the handkerchief cannot be paralleled by Iago's loss of a real battle flag. Iago loses merely the sign of a sign, his title, which he does not really lose but willingly surrenders in return for another: "Now art thou my lieutenant" . . . "I am your own forever."

Iago's passage from ancient to lieutenant is a passage from sign to substitute; now he no longer signifies the Moor's identity but assumes it, functioning "in lieu of" the general. Othello's outward signifier fuses with his inward signified as he makes Iago his own, and of course as Iago makes Othello *his* own. If Iago as ancient had seemed an arbitrary sign of the general's identity, with a stress on difference, he now becomes a natural sign, with a stress on resemblance. Their "marriage" is a form of semiotic bonding that has overtones of demonic possession. Signs have thus taken a grotesquely proper revenge on Othello, insofar as his nobly natural impulse has been to assume that signifiers and signifieds *are* indissoluble, that words and meanings are wedded to one another in the most literal of senses.

2. The Narrative Subject

If the ensign may become the general whose sign he is, and if signifiers may become their signifieds, then surely the style may be the man. Our bodies tell us and others who we are—our bodies and especially what our bodies do and how they do it, their physical style. Who can mistake Magic Johnson's headlong orchestration of a three-on-two fast break, Itzhak Perlman's agonizings at the violin, or Ronald Reagan's smiling, waving, miming regretful deafness to reporters' questions as he makes for Air Force One? But of course the most distinctive thing our bodies do is speak. And if speech is incorrigibly common by virtue of the repeatability of words, voices and verbal styles are blessedly uncommon. Voice prints will identify us as readily as fingerprints, and Othello's style of speech rings distinctively familiar in everyone's ear.[6]

Othello descants the Othello music, those arias of splendid sonority that rise and fall like the stormy waters off Cyprus and sometimes flow as inexorably as the Pontic Sea.[7] In his mouth, casual greetings take on the character of sacred vows, and even when he confesses himself rough with words he does so in the accents of Demosthenes:[8]

> Rude am I in my speech,
> And little blessed with the soft phrase of peace;
> For since these arms of mine had seven years' pith,
> Till now some nine moons wasted, they have used
> Their dearest action in the tented field;
> And little of this great world can I speak
> More than pertains to feats of broil and battle,
> And therefore little shall I grace my cause
> In speaking for myself.   (1.3.83)

By Act 4, however, we will find ourselves saying "That's he that was Othello. Here he is":

> Lie with her? Lie on her? We say lie on her, when they belie her. Lie with her! 'Zounds, that's fulsome.—Handkerchief—confessions—handkerchief!—To confess, and be hanged for his labor—first, to be hanged, and then to confess.—I tremble at it. Nature would not invest herself in such shadowing passion without some instruction. It is not words that shakes me thus. Pish! Noses, ears, and lips.—Is it possible?—Confess—handkerchief!—O devil!

These are the first lines of prose Othello utters—surely, one would think, a significant moment. To see just how significant, however, requires a context. Let us return to his verse self and better times.

In the opening act, Othello is in command of speech, and at first his speeches are mostly commands: "Holla, stand there!" . . . "Keep up your bright swords." . . . "Hold your hands" (1.2). He is so sure of himself that he is willing to obey Brabantio and proceed to the Senate, where amid the nervous scurryings of rumor his speech stands out in its calm confidence, most notably when he assumes the role of narrator in response to the Duke's invitation "Say it, Othello" (129). Since Othello's self-exonerating speeches here are central to his concept of self, let us consider them and him in terms of narrative and monologue.

In effect Othello says "She willingly came with me." But in his mouth nothing is ever that simple. "She willingly came" is transformed into an extended account of his oblique courtship of Desdemona, which consisted of his saying, as heroic lovers often do, "Here I am, Othello. Let me tell you the meaning of that name, and you will love me." Of all Shakespeare's characters, Othello testifies most thoroughly to the fact that everyone is a biography, a life-story constantly being written and revised, told and retold. As the neurologist Oliver Sacks observes, "Biologically, physiologically, we are not so different from each other; historically, as narratives—we are each of us unique."[9] This is more than usually true of the Moor because as a "wheeling stranger / Of here and everywhere" he cannot rely, as Venetians can, on the unity of residential place to lend coherence to his life—what Kenneth Burke would call a "scene-agent ratio" (you *are* by virtue of where you are).[10] Instead he must continually re-establish his sense of self narratively. Thus not only is he telling himself at this moment before the Senate, but the subject of his telling is further tellings. His story about his courtship of Desdemona is recursively suspended to admit in evidence the stories of which that courtship consisted.[11] For a moment we seem on the edge of an *Arabian Nights* infinite recursion whereby Shakespeare's dramatic story yields to Othello's senatorial story, which yields to his courtship stories of cannibals and Anthropophagi, which might perhaps yield to . . . But fortunately do not.

This narrative in which the narrator is in several senses the "subject" gives us a divided perspective on Othello. In the first place, as story-telling subject or seemingly autonomous self, he is present and in command of the scene, exercising such dominion over shifters as to transform *I* into his own proper name, while everyone else is distanced and subordinated to the status of *he* or *she*. All words and meanings come under his monopoly; the capitalist of self is also the capitalist of speech who puts words profitably to work to earn Desdemona's love and the Senate's approval.[12] He imposes his image of himself on others through sheer force of continuity, his meanings rolling rhetorically forth in sentences of such sustained syntactic complexity that he might be writing instead of speaking, since he is no more subject to interruption than the author of a treatise.

In these respects, as storyteller in the Senate, Othello aggrandizes himself as subject. Moreover, because of the recursiveness of his story, because he is a voice telling about himself telling about himself, his possession of the *I* is reaffirmed within his own story. Normally, that is, the *I* that speaks and the *I* that is spoken, although they tend to merge in the imagination, are demonstrably discrete, the former being the speaking subject, the latter the grammatical subject.[13] In fact the grammatical "subject" has an element of the accusative about it, inasmuch as it is not merely the doer of verbal deeds within each sentence but the done-unto, the object of the speaking subject's speech. Othello, however, fends off this accusative element, keeping it at one further remove by mirroring and embedding the speaking subject in the grammatical one. The *I* who is spoken about is also a speaker telling stories to Desdemona. It's not until we get to the *I* who stands for the adventurous hero, instead of for the speaking voice, that Othello takes on an accusative aspect—appropriately, for instance, in his brief mention of having been "taken by the insolent foe" and sold to slavery, an embarrassing occasion in which his being physically enslaved is analogous to his enthrallment to the words of his own speech.

Thus the act of telling about himself subtly subverts Othello's domination of speech and, through speech, his domination of the Senate and of Desdemona and Brabantio earlier. After all, his life is being recast in verbal forms. He says that he ran through his biography for Brabantio "even from my very boyish days / To the very moment that he bade me tell it" (1.3.134) and that at Desdemona's request he later dilated on "all [his] pilgrimage" (155). But the story of his life does not stop there; even now before the Senate a further episode is being appended, "Othello's Courtship of Desdemona." Normally the speaking subject is enormously in excess of the grammatical subject; we *are* far more than we can say. But so great is the stress on Othello's representations of himself that the events of his life seem lived just one Shandy-like step ahead of the words that seize and digest them into story.

This near-fusion of Othello and his life story entails a special vulnerability. His identity is as riskily entrusted to narrative signs here as it is to the flag and handkerchief borne by his two ensigns, Iago and Desdemona. Add to this the fact that Othello's distinctive *style*, which from one perspective is inseparably specific to him, from another perspective marks his speech as rhetorically fashioned and hence separable from him, and we see that what seems most natural to him is also most alien from him. Thus if the structure of his self is so exclusively constituted by the structure of his speech, then to destroy Othello you need merely put his language on the rack. Bastinado his diction, twist his syntax. Make him say "Lie with her? Lie on her? We say lie on her, when they belie her. Lie with her! 'Zounds, that's fulsome.—Handkerchief—confessions—handkerchief!" and his body is at your mercy.

Thus Othello is at double risk. His identity, which ought by rights to exceed his speech, is dangerously confined and entrusted to it. Even at its moment of greatest power before the Senate, his speech unavoidably splits him into a speaking and a spoken *I*—perhaps the first suggestion we have of the fission of self that will later cause Desdemona to say "My lord is not my lord" (3.4.125).[14]

3. Signs and De-Signs

In light of the fact that Brabantio, Desdemona, and now the Senate have succumbed to his eloquence, it is little wonder Othello puts his faith in words. Like Harry Hotspur, another romantic warrior, he is a platonic idealist for whom abstractions have a worshipful reality. Hotspur's favorite abstraction is *honor*, Othello's is *honest*.[15] For him *honest* is a transcendental signifier that stabilizes discourse; he believes not only in the word *honest* but in the honesty of words. Although he speaks the language of high romance,[16] he naively assumes that even the most ethereal of words are bonded to their meanings and those meanings bonded in turn to what they represent. Call Iago honest and he *is* honest. Which means that honest Iago has only to pin the word *dishonest* securely on Desdemona to guarantee her death.

Iago is honest enough to say "The Moor is of a free and open nature, / That thinks men honest that but seem to be so" (1.3.400). The Moor's logocentrism extends to his judgment of people. For him, a person is like a sign in which signifier and signified are paired by nature; what you see is what you get. Iago's blunt straightforward manner and Desdemona's beauty are reliable indices of honesty and virtue. Even the naive Desdemona is more subtly Venetian in this respect than Othello: she saw the Moor's visage in his mind, disregarding the black signifiers without—although on the other hand she is like him in taking his stories about himself at face value.

Not that Othello is content with signifiers. He trustingly accepts *seems* for *so*, but it is the *so*, the signified within, that he seeks. Thus when Iago's vaguenesses begin to stir in his imagination, his first reaction is to brush aside words and get to the unmediated thing itself: "If thou dost love me," he demands of Iago, "Show me thy thought" (3.3.120). Still, even here he has not dispensed with mediation entirely; Iago's hidden thought must somehow be "shown," even in words:

> I prithee speak to me as to thy thinkings,
> As thou dost ruminate, and give thy worst of thoughts
> The worst of words. (3.3.136)

The following fifty or so lines play increasingly passionate variations on this theme, building up to Othello's angry "By heaven, I'll know thy thoughts!" (3.3.166). By this time mediation disappears; he would understand Iago's mind not as mortal men are obliged to do, by reason and discourse, but as angels (and perhaps devils) do, by instinct or intuition.

Unfortunately Iago refuses to speak, and Othello lacks clairvoyance. Honesty grows suspect; it is not what it is. If Iago is honest and speaks out, then Cassio and Desdemona will surely prove dishonest; whereas as long as he is dishonestly secretive, they remain honest in name, whatever they may be in fact. No wonder Othello says "What dost thou mean?" What Iago means, he says, is that he is something of an idealist himself, claiming in Cassio-like terms that "who steals my purse steals trash" but "he that filches from me my good name" steals true value (3.3.160–65). Therefore he will not speak his thoughts.

What is Othello to make of this? Honest Iago is unforthcomingly dishonest, yet for noble reasons that make him seem more deeply honest than if he had spoken straight out. With Iago's honesty apparently growing in proportion to his dishonesty, no wonder Othello is puzzled and frustrated.

By this time Iago's insinuations have set Othello adrift on a sea of deconstructive signifiers in accordance with the sign theory Iago proclaimed earlier to Roderigo: "I must show out a flag and sign of love, / Which is indeed but sign" (1.1.158). Iago's style is to run up flags and signs that can be switched at a moment's notice. In fact his signs are really "designs" in a double sense, a kind of deconstructive scheming, inasmuch as they "de-sign" or divest signs of meaning in order to fulfill his villainous designs. The sign for him is a one-sided coin, signifier up; its signified, the thought that could make the coin's face value good (or in this case bad), is nowhere to be found. Iago's worst words can express no worst thoughts, for the simple reason that he has no worst thoughts; he knows perfectly well that Desdemona and Cassio are above suspicion. Unanchored either to referents or to signifieds, his insinuations float free, deferring meaning indefinitely and obliging Othello to drift on an endless current of suggestion.

4. Ocular Proof and Body Language

If Othello cannot gain access to Iago's conclusive thoughts by way of words, how then? The answer is simple and familiar; the epistemology of the West rests on it: merely look. "To be once in doubt," Othello says, "is once to be resolved," and the way to be resolved, as the empiricists especially argued, is to follow the optic nerve:

> I'll see before I doubt; when I doubt, prove;
> And on the proof, there is no more but this—
> Away at once with love or jealousy. (3.3.196)

This is more famously expressed later when he collars Iago and demands "Villain, be sure thou prove my love a whore! Be sure of it. Give me the ocular proof" (3.3.364), after which, just to be sure there is no mistake, he adds,

> Make me to see it, or at the least so prove it
> That the probation bear no hinge nor loop
> To hang a doubt on; or woe upon thy life! (369)

Clearly the eye's the thing wherein he'll catch the conscience of the quean. To break free of slippery signifiers like *honesty* and gain access to the unmediated truth, he will dismiss words altogether and take the incomparably honest eye to friend.

Iago seizes on the idea with enthusiasm. First he ocularizes his language, painting lascivious images of Cassio and Desdemona in the fiction of the dreaming Cassio (415–30). When Othello begins to rage, Iago both taunts him by complaining "Yet we see nothing done"—as though the game were too easily won—"She may be honest yet"

(436). Then he leads Othello, still with no more than a noose of
words, to the terrible speech quoted earlier in which he falls from
verse into prose:

> Lie with her? Lie on her? We say lie on her, when they belie her. Lie
> with her! 'Zounds, that's fulsome.—Handkerchief—confessions—
> handkerchief!—To confess, and be hanged for his labor—first, to be
> hanged, and then to confess.—I tremble at it. Nature would not
> invest herself in such shadowing passion without some instruction. It
> is not words that shakes me thus. Pish! Noses, ears, and lips.—Is it
> possible?—Confess—handkerchief!—O devil!

If Othello simply fell from verse to prose here it would be startling
enough, but in fact he plunges right on through prose to a series of
incoherent cries and babblings at the edge of the sublinguistic. In
view of his earlier sublimations of language, his logocentric concern
for signifieds, it is ironic that his discourse should be reduced to a
random play of signifiers alone. Now he is caught up in the low
material stuff that words are made on, the carnal body of sounds
stripped of sense.

Thus Shakespeare draws a painful parallel between Othello's
(non) language and his (non) love. In the Senate Scene earlier, recoil-
ing almost in disgust from the notion that he might want to take
Desdemona to Cyprus for sexual reasons, Othello purified his wife
Lady Macbeth-like, by unsexing her there, and then. If we say as so
many critics have, either in praise or complaint, that Othello's love is
idealistic and lacks body, then in this scene that metaphor unmeta-
phors itself. Desdemona becomes not a body to bed but a soul to
enfranchise ("to be free and bounteous to her mind" [1.3.268]), a
Petrarchan divinity inviting allegorization as the antithesis to Iago's
diabolism, which is characterized by a misogynistic obsession with
the repellancies of the body. That antithesis moves toward a degrading synthesis, however, when Othello becomes convinced of Desdemona's villainy. Then he too sees evil in her body, particularly in the
hand into which his kerchief was entrusted; "This hand," he observes, "is moist, my lady" (3.4.36), adding a gloss on moistness:

> This argues fruitfulness and liberal heart.
> Hot, hot, and moist. This hand of yours requires
> A sequester from liberty, fasting and prayer,
> Much castigation, exercise devout;
> For here's a young and sweating devil here

> That commonly rebels. 'Tis a good hand,
> And a frank one.

'Tis a good hand, not morally but semiotically, a synecdochic sign that frankly announces the presence of a young and sweating devil. That Othello the reborn Christian regards the body as devilish we might have suspected from his puritanical rejection of sexual pleasure in the Senate Scene, but now the demonic equation emerges clearly, forecasting the necessity of exorcism.

Before that, however, we see Desdemona's divinity and Othello's style collapse together. In his disjointed speech, he is assaulted by images of her as a body to be lain with or on, and then finally as no more than a repellant concatenation of physical parts—"Noses, ears, and lips."[17] Everything descends not merely to body here but rather, as in a *sparagmos*, to a torn and dismembered body. Noses, ears, and lips are to the intact physique as Othello's fragmented utterance is to authentic syntax—indeed as Othello's own trembling and shaking limbs at this moment are to his fine physical presence in earlier scenes. What issues from Othello is not romantic verse or even plain prose but something not quite speech, a verbal epilepsy—a regression from language in its abstract and symbolic role as the instrument of godlike reason to language as the almost preverbal Artaud-like noises expelled by a creature in pain.[18]

When Othello falls into his epilepsy one further parallel ensues, for his seizure consists of an obliteration of consciousness and a consequent deterioration of reflective man to that state which Hamlet called bestial oblivion. The idealistic Othello to whom the bodily and material are a source of corruption—to whom love must be ethereally chaste or else, the only imaginable alternative, "a cistern for foul toads to knot and gender in!" (4.2.61)—is now reduced to nothing but body, a lump of quivering matter. And if the body is the Devil's empire, as Luther maintained, and Iago is at least a demi-devil, then Othello and Desdemona are now most perilously abandoned within His Satanic Majesty's dominion.[19]

5. The Storied Self

Othello clearly can go no further in this verbal direction. Despite his sinking cry "It is not words that shakes me thus," it is still precisely words that shakes him thus. It is past time to shift to ocular proofs, for the eye is incorruptibly honest. Iago obliges by staging the play-within, at last bringing forth for inspection his secret thoughts, not in slippery phrases and vague insinuations but open and palpable as a pageant. Now at last Othello is satisfied. There in full and damning sight are the smiling Cassio, the beckoning Iago, the embraces, then Cassio's whore, and finally the handkerchief itself (4.1.105–68). In keeping with his own prescription for revenge, he has seen, doubted, proved, and there is no more but this: "How shall I murder him, Iago?" (4.1.169).

However, what Iago knows and Othello does not is that ocular proofs are no more transcendental and unmediated than verbal ones:

> As [Cassio] shall smile, Othello shall go mad;
> And his unbookish jealousy must conster
> Poor Cassio's smiles, gestures, and light behavior
> Quite in the wrong. (4.1.101)

Here Iago rather brilliantly translates the visual into the verbal to demonstrate that the observing eye is not all that different from the reading eye (or the hearing ear). Iago employs space as a blank sheet on which he writes his lubricous meanings with the stylus of Cassio's smiles, gestures, and light behavior. And Othello, convinced that he is simply registering the naked phenomenological truth, reads what Iago has written, and misconsters all. No surprises there. Othello is, after all, an unbookish barbarian; the subtleties of mediation undo him quite. Thus he stands apart, entering his crude glosses in the margins of Iago's fleeting text—"Now he denies it faintly, and laughs it out. . . . Do you triumph, Roman? . . . By heaven, that should be my handkerchief!" Even afterwards when Iago remarks upon the handkerchief and he is obliged to ask "Was that mine?" he still believes he has been recording the unmediated truth. And because he does, he chooses to regard Desdemona herself as a fair paper and goodly book in which Cassio has written the word *whore* (4.2.71).

These bookish metaphors call to mind the role played by printing in the development of Western capitalism.

> [Book publishing] was one of the first industries that required a capital investment to procure the means of production. It was also one of the first enterprises in which speculation played a prominent role. Publishing involved the marketing of a mass-manufactured product. It was a highly competitive field, where price was dictated by the laws of supply and demand.[20]

More important, Marshall McLuhan claims that the book as "portable commodity" created the price system: "For until commodities are uniform and repeatable the price of an article is subject to haggle and adjustment."[21] Thus we might argue that the introduction of book metaphors in *Othello*, and especially that in which Desdemona is represented as a book written in by the "pens" of other men, suggests the reduction of the unique and privately owned Desdemona to a repeatable commodity, as portable and purchasable a piece of goods as a book. The commonness of the book parallels the commonness of the money for which Roderigo trades his land and whores market their favors.

In any event, interpreting Iago's stagy inscriptions drives the unlearned Othello mad, as Iago predicted. Not mad like Lear: it is a measure of his delusion that we must put his "madness" within quotation marks, as we do Desdemona's "dishonesty." Whereas Lear, casting aside his protective cultural clothing, is battered into honest madness by the true immediacy of the storm, Othello is driven "mad" by the pseudo-storms of Iago's mediated stagings.[22] Still, the storm within Othello is real enough to overwhelm the sense he struggles to retain. Out of the whirlwind of his passion Desdemona hears words that are both demeaning and demeaned, signifiers that no longer signify:

> Upon my knees, what doth your speech import?
> I understand a fury in your words,
> But not the words. (4.2.31)

After this he curses her in the presence of Lodovico, strikes her, and banishes her from his presence.

Following his epileptic speech, Othello's syntax improves, but his meanings still twitch furiously until Act 4, Scene 3 and Emilia's ominous comment to Desdemona, "How goes it now? He looks gentler than he did" (11). The calm, if not gentleness, of his manner reoccurs in the Murder Scene, which recapitulates in small the larger fall of Othello's speech throughout the play. Diapasons of his former style and stately rhythms reappear as he enters now intoning "It is the cause." As self-assured as he was at his first entrance, he addresses himself to a respiritualized Desdemona whose soul, heaven forfend, he would not kill. Indeed he is even willing to take auricular confession. But when she remains simply a loving woman instead of a contrite fallen nun, Othello's style falters and then fails him altogether. "Alas," Desdemona cries, "why gnaw you so your nether lip? / Some bloody passion shakes your very frame"—just as it did during his seizure. His words grow increasingly abusive as his frustration mounts, until at last he seizes on murder as a kind of manual correlative to ocular proof—a transcendental signified meant to terminate the play of speech: "But while I say one prayer!" . . . "It is too late."

The last phase of Othello's story is another story, beginning "Soft you; a word or two before you go." In his early stories about himself, he was subsumed by narrative, simultaneously telling and being told. So it is again at the end. He hushes other speakers to convert them into an audience of his own speech. Once again he becomes the speaking *I*—but also the subject to be spoken of, not only by himself but by his audience. He must speak to them because it is they who will speak of him: "Speak of me as I am." And then, typically, he tells their story for them—

> Then must you speak
> Of one that loved not wisely but too well;
> Of one not easily jealous, but, being wrought,
> Perplex'd in the extreme; of one whose hand,
> Like the base Indian, threw a pearl away
> Richer than all his tribe; of one whose subdued eyes,
> Albeit unused to the melting mood,
> Drops tears as fast as the Arabian trees
> Their medicinable gum. Set you down this;
> And say besides, that in Aleppo once,
> Where a malignant and a turban'd Turk
> Beat a Venetian and traduc'd the state,
> I took by th' throat the circumcised dog,
> And smote him, thus.

Just as he told his life story up to the moment Brabantio asked him to tell it, and continued it up to the moment the Duke said "Say it, Othello," so now he resumes the tale, bringing his life up to date and providing us with a brief chronicle of the play itself. If his life has always been lived just a breath ahead of his stories about himself, now life and story terminally coincide at the moment of death: "O bloody period!" Lodovico exclaims as the dagger makes its fatal point. When Gratiano adds "All that is spoke is marred," his words suggest not merely that Othello's suicide casts a foul light on his fine words but that his bloody period has blotted the fair written page of his self. Inasmuch as he is both the speaker and "all that is spoke," his assimilation to story is complete.

6. Monologue/Dialogue

Othello's narrative monopoly on language in the first act and his subsequent loss of that monopoly during his verbal exchanges with Iago suggest that Mikhail Bakhtin's views about monologue and dialogue may provide a means of making helpful distinctions between the two.[23] Taking that perspective, let us see how the play looks.

As noted earlier, Othello's speech bears some similarities to writing. For instance when he speaks in monologue he commands language as a writer does when he writes. The high formality of his opening lines—"Most potent, grave, and reverend signiors, / My very noble and approved good masters"—reserves a solemn and sizable space for his holding forth. The assurance that he will proceed without interruption allows him amplitude of utterance. He can afford the large phrase and sustained period, the rhythms of repetition, the crafting of parallels, subordinations, parentheses, antitheses, and the lingering evocations of detail that help unfold his rhetorical plot from that opening apostrophe to the formal closure of "This only is the witchcraft I have used."

All of this unhurried stylizing of speech has a greater affinity to writing than to utterance. This affinity appears also in Othello's near total investment of meaning in words alone. When he tells his story, nothing is assumed, everything is said. Once under way, his words roll on autonomously, indifferent to their immediate nonverbal context, each sentence responding to the thrust of the one before it and preparing the way for the one following it. Like most forms of public address, Othello's speech is designed not to further dialogue but to suspend it. As a performance, the proper response to it is applause, which is just what it gets: "I think this tale would win my daughter too."

In Act 3, however, Othello finds himself in Iago's dialogistic territory, a place of disjunctive utterances and echoings, of eyebrows raised and fingers laid along the nose, of musings meant to be overheard and silences loud with implication. Meaning resides now in the unspoken aspects of the scene or immediate context even more than it does in words. With Iago, the unsaid always says more than the said.

The thrust of speech comes not syntactically from within as in monologue, where phrases and sentences build on their predecessors, but
responsively from without, each utterance answering one before it
and preparing for one to follow, a reply that invites a reply, as when
Iago repeats Othello's words in the form of a question—"Honest, my
lord?" "Think, my lord?" The extent to which meaning arises from
the scene—this speaker, this audience, this shared subject, this
known past and anticipated future—is suggested by Iago's sly employment of deictics and demonstratives. "Ha! I like not *that*," he
begins (3.3.35); or "scan *this thing* no farther; leave *it* to time"
(3.3.252) and "I see, sir, that you are eaten up with passion. / I do
repent me that I put *it* to you" (3.3.396). Such terms, meaningless in
themselves, imply a shared understanding and a community of interest: we two, here and now, faced with this difficulty, knowing what we
know.

The irony lies in the fact that Iago is inviting Othello out of his
fortress of monologue into a social scene where he must share his *I*,
honor the verbal rights of others, and cultivate a negative capability.
Such projections and outgoings should have been implicit in his love
for Desdemona, but of course we have seen how much Othello's love
went forth only in search of his own reflection and how constitutionally opposed to dialogue his famous style is. Monologue makes its
own meaning, and Othello's verbal idealism lodges all meaning in
words.[24] Obliged to attend to meanings situated, or in Iago's slick
practice seemingly situated, outside language, in silence, in undi-
vulged thought, in pitch and accent and smiles and nods and hand-
kerchiefs, and perhaps most of all in such "common knowledge" as
the sly sexual maneuvers of Venetian ladies (3.3.207–10), Othello
breaks down.

But after all what should we have expected? The Moor is a
stranger. He is not privy to the world shared by Venetians: the social
order, habits, standards, expectations, all that stands behind the
simplest remark one person makes to another, guaranteeing that what
is meant by the one is at least roughly what is understood by the other.
He always speaks from a place outside of at the borders of this
cultural scene. Perfectly natural, then, that he should situate as much
meaning as possible in words, and especially in his own words. To
grasp meanings lying outside and around and behind words he is
dependent on those in the know. And of course Iago is always in the
know. Othello's cry "By heaven, I'll know thy thought" stands
beside his bemused comment "Dost thou say so?" (3.3.211) as testi-

mony to a desire that can never be wholly satisfied by the stranger, the knowledge that is simply known, the understanding that is understood, all that is given to Venetians because of experiences shared while Othello was engineering hairbreadth escapes off in antres vast and deserts idle.

In light of these considerations, the Murder Scene is a mockery of dialogue. Othello enters in the old vein, intoning his music, fashioning a lyric poem about the finalities of death; and although what follows has the appearance of dialogue, especially in the stichomythic exchanges, everything Othello says is designed to impose his own exclusive interpretation on the occasion and to prevent further speech. Cassio's "mouth is stopped" (74), and so should Desdemona's be: "Peace, and be still!" (48). Desdemona is cast in the role of questioner, inviting response, and Othello as answerer, having the final word. Even when she prays, it is he who utters "Amen," setting the conventional verbal seal on her words:

DES.   Then heaven
       Have mercy on me!
OTH.   Amen, with all my heart!
DES.   Then Lord have mercy on me!
OTH.   I say, amen.

Amen puts a period to prayer as a period puts an end to a sentence; and inasmuch as we hear Desdemona repeatedly beginning lines that Othello concludes—as in the examples just cited—he is literally the periodic end-stop of dialogistic verse. This is increasingly the case as the scene moves on —

DES.   Let [Cassio] confess a truth.
OTH.   He hath confessed.
DES.   What, my lord?
OTH.   That he hath used thee.
DES.   How? Unlawfully?
OTH.   Ay.

—until it reaches its unhappy climax when Othello puts a terminal end-stop to her speech:

DES.   But half an hour!
OTH.   Being done, there is no pause.
DES.   But while I say one prayer.
OTH.   It is too late.

Smothers her.

Othello may stop Cassio's mouth and then Desdemona's, but human affairs are incorrigibly dialogistic; there is always an Emilia at the door crying "My lord, my lord! What ho! My lord, my lord!" and demanding that the world outside be allowed to speak its disruptive piece. What the world says is that Othello is a murdering fool. And Othello—what does he say?

That is, after all this playing-off of monologue against dialogue, how should we understand Othello's last speech? Has he profited stylistically from his experience? Perhaps. The speech is a monologue of sorts, an attempt to redefine himself and bring to a final close, a bloody period, both his words and his life. Yet it is also open-ended, not merely acknowledging but relying on the subsequent speech of others ("Then must you speak"), and as it were open-beginninged in that it issues from prior speech ("Soft you") and comments on what has gone before ("these unlucky deeds"). Moreover, as that definite description suggests—perhaps with a gesture in the direction of Desdemona—it takes its source in the immediate context and is grounded in common knowledge ("I have done the state some service, and they know it. / No more of that"). Finally its most significant meaning derives not from words alone, as in the Senate Scene, but from an act that can be known for certain only if you are there to see it, since it is represented verbally by nothing more enlightening than "thus." To be sure, the deed emerges from the words "I took by the throat the circumcised dog, / And smote him, thus," but without the stage direction *Stabs himself* an actor or director reading the script might momentarily assume that Othello is supposed to seize and stab Iago, or even Lodovico or Gratiano.

Perhaps the merger of monologue and dialogue in the speech does justice to Othello's insistence on asserting his distinctive status as tragic hero, which allows him to say the last word himself ("O bloody period!"), while at the same time registering his chastened awareness that he is about to become merely words in the mouths of other men, a phrasal link in an endless chain of utterance.

Othello's Occupation:
The Evils of Nobility

I. Shadowed Ideals

In the middle of Act 3, Scene 3, the distraught Othello delivers his famous and rather surprising speech bidding farewell to his occupation (3.3.352–62). How content he could have been, he has been saying, if only he had known nothing of "her stolen hours of lust" (343):

> I had been happy if the general camp,
> Pioners and all, had tasted her sweet body,
> So I had nothing known. O, now, forever
> Farewell the tranquil mind! Farewell content!
> Farewell the plumed troop, and the big wars
> That makes ambition virtue! O, farewell!
> Farewell the neighing steed, and the shrill trump,
> The spirit-stirring drum, the ear-piercing fife,
> The royal banner, and all quality,
> Pride, pomp, and circumstance of glorious war!
> And, O you mortal engines, whose rude throats
> The immortal Jove's dread clamors counterfeit,
> Farewell! Othello's occupation's gone.

To which Iago: "Is it possible, my lord?" And Othello, returning to the point:

> Villain, be sure thou prove my love a whore!
> Be sure of it. Give me the ocular proof.

Othello's farewell speech is surprising because it is by no means clear why the loss of a wife should entail the loss of a soldierly occupation. Moreover, the context here is so replete with talk about whoring that the valediction to warfare seems additionally out of place. What we might have expected is a lament for the loss of Desdemona: "Farewell to ruby lips and azure eyes" etc. Even if war *is* somehow relevant, why should it be renounced? In a similar situation, the betrayed Troilus, far from abdicating his military business, wants nothing better than to rampage after Greeks in the field.

Actually the Moor's lament tells us something important about both the play and its critics. To begin with, we should note the bitter pun with which the speech ends, for Othello's "occupation" is not only military but sexual. That a highminded speech on the glories of war should conduct us to a bawdy pun on the General's eviction from his phallic residence is something of a disgrace, but there you are. Not only there you are but there you typically are, because throughout the play Shakespeare makes a practice of smuggling the sordid and sexual across property lines inside the luggage of the romantic and idealistic. This tactic works to perfection in that, apart from Iago, none of the characters takes note of it—very much as few critics and far fewer playgoers register the bawdy meaning of *occupation*.[1]

Criticism of *Othello*, as everyone knows, divides into those who find the Moor admirably noble—for example, A. C. Bradley, Helen Gardner, John Bayley, John Holloway, and Reuben Brower— and those who regard him as deeply flawed—for example, T. S. Eliot, F. R. Leavis, Allardyce Nicoll, Leo Kirschbaum, and Robert B. Heilman.[2] Perhaps a partial reconciliation of these views might be effected if we admitted on the one hand that the Moor *is* deeply flawed and on the other that his flaw is his nobility. The trouble with nobility is that it is noble. A kind of unmoved mover, nobility transcends the ordinary and merely human: it disdains the cannon shot that puffs brothers away, walks cooly past men whose heads do grow between their shoulders, and dashes aside bright swords and street brawls in Venice. It takes the principled high way. And while its eyes are on the stars, like Swift's philosopher, it is very often seduced by its lower parts into a ditch—or, like Othello, into tragic delusions. Why? Because in its fastidiousness nobility will leave the dirty work of getting the goods on one's wife to people like Iago—"Villain, be sure thou prove my love a whore!"—and in its altitudinous impartiality it will say things like "Cassio, I love thee; / But never more be officer of mine" and "It is the cause, it is the cause, my soul." Nobility can love Cassio but cashier him anyhow, and kiss Desdemona but kill her nonetheless.

But there is a certain justice in this, because Cassio and Desdemona are themselves as noble and idealistic as the Moor. It is Cassio, after all, whose lamentations about the loss of his immortal reputation generates Iago's contemptuous "As I am an honest man, I thought you had received some bodily wound" (2.3.260).[3] If *reputation* and *soul* are synonyms in Cassio's lexicon, and if Desdemona is "a maid / That paragons description and wild fame" (2.1.63), then in what lofty celestial rank does her soul reside? Surely in some angelic order, for to "[see] Othello's visage in his mind," as she says she did, requires more than human discernment. Here is love in its most disembodied form. Othello's black skin, "thick lips," and aging body are merely a window through which Desdemona spies the platonic essence or inner visage of his virtue.[4]

Of course Othello takes much the same line. Indeed he takes the same word, *visage*, when he says that

> Her name, that was as fresh
> As Dian's visage, is now begrimed and black
> As mine own face. (3.3.391)

To describe even her degraded state, he calls on platonic phrases. Although he takes account of a visage here, it is the never-seen visage of a goddess, not Desdemona's. *Her* face he metaphorically transforms into a name, a detached verbal essence analogous to Cassio's soulful reputation.

It remains for Iago to bring these matters down to earth—to begrime names, reputations, and faces and indeed anything he can touch. That he is at hand for such business illustrates the familiar fact that in Shakespeare all bright ideals cast shadows. Whenever a character or action strains at the upward limits of what men and women are and do, a return of the repressed takes place, usually in language—in words like *occupation*, for instance, or Desdemona's *abhor*. Language has little truck with idealistic purity. Something of a whore itself in its public traffic, speech revolts against chastity and, Iago-like, says the unspeakable. Iago shadows Othello the way *whore* and *foin* shadow "abhor" and "occupy."[5]

But these dark meanings pass unremarked by the noble characters in the play, just as the villainous Iago passes unremarked in the honest Iago. As that suggests, Iago is also a kind of obscene pun, a bawdy evil meaning that is continually given voice, yet that goes as unheard by the other characters as his soliloquies do. Up to a point, then, *Othello* reveals to us the cost of being noble. The cost is Iago. If you want to be noble you must repress Iago. That means you must repress a certain honesty, because if Othello is noble, Iago is honest—or at least he is "honest." He expresses what Othello represses; he tells the truths the rest of us lie about in order to claim some measure of decency if not nobility. He says "I hate the Moor" *before* finding reasons for it, admits to acting on "mere suspicion," sneers at Cassio as "a proper man," wants to "plume up [his] will" in knavery, tries on lies as he would cheveril gloves, acknowledges a gnawing jealousy and an appetite for revenge, thinks of women as sexual property, exposes his fears of his own littleness beside Othello and Cassio, and assumes that when his desires are impeded his natural recourse is murder, even if the impediment is his wife.

I don't mean that Iago is an allegorical sign of Othello's unconscious. He *is* that in some degree, but he is also the unconscious of the play itself; or, in dramaturgical terms, he is all that Shakespeare the playwright felt obliged to exclude when he fashioned characters like Othello, Desdemona, and Cassio. That means that Iago is somewhat within them by virtue of being kept outside of them; or at least he is indispensable to them, since they are nobly what they are by virtue of not being ignoble like him. He is a kind of theatrical residue of Shakespeare's creation of nobility. A romantic playwright might have discarded this residue entirely, but Shakespeare not merely retains it but makes it into a character with enormous theatrical vitality, the conscious unconscious of the play, appropriately voicing his knavish honesty in soliloquy and aside.

At one extreme, the objective and overt, we have the nobility of Othello's public speeches. They rise idealistically above the plane of dialogic give and take, almost shaming ordinary language into silence with their high-minded sonority. At the other extreme, the subjective and covert, are Iago's soliloquies. Iago's, not Othello's—because Othello never speaks in soliloquy; everything with him is outward and upward. Iago's soliloquies are honest because they publish, albeit quietly, everything Othello's speeches suppress. From their perspective, Othello's noble claims are all bombast and vaunt, just as from Othello's perspective (were he less myopic) Iago's ignobilities are all lies. Stylistically in between these two modes, pulled magnetically now this way, now that, is the speech of people like Desdemona, Cassio, Brabantio, Roderigo, Emilia, and to be sure the nonsoliloquizing Iago and the nonspeechifying Othello. This is the region where truth and lies mix confusedly, where Desdemona can lie twice and Othello once, where Iago sometimes tells truths when he speaks and almost always lies when he says nothing, and where no one can sort out the two until the end.[6]

From this perspective, the central action of the play is the desublimation of Othello, or the unrepression of Iago. This movement takes quasi-allegorical form in Othello's divorce from Desdemona and his remarriage to Iago, which releases his repressed capacity for violence. It is signaled also by the disappearance of Iago's soliloquies after Act 2—or rather their release from subjectivity, because Iago's repressed "truths" rise to the surface of the play when Othello gives credence to his innuendoes. On the principle that where *ego* was, let *id* be, the scurrilities of soliloquy acquire a public voice first in Iago's sidelong suggestions and then in the accusations and rant of the Moor. The climactic point of verbal desublimation occurs when the "Othello music" turns cacophonic in the epileptic speech of Act 4, Scene 1—"It is not words that shake me thus. Pish! Noses, ears, and lips"—which is accompanied by a very literal loss of consciousness as *ego* yields to *id*.

But just what is it the noble Moor has repressed?

2. Manly Properties: War and Immortality

For one thing, Othello represses or at least suppresses sexual desire. In the Senate Scene when Desdemona asks to accompany her husband to Cyprus, she modestly but forthrightly expresses an interest in "the rites for why I love him" (1.3.260). Othello seconds her request, but in a speech that rivals the sleepwalking Lady Macbeth in its concern for sanitation. He wants it clearly known that he married not to bed a wife—a practice which deploring Puritans regarded as tantamount to visiting a brothel[7]—but to enjoy the rarer congress of true minds:

> Vouch with me, heaven, I therefore beg it not
> To please the palate of my appetite,
> Nor to comply with heat—the young affects
> In me defunct—and proper satisfaction,
> But to be free and bounteous to her mind. . . .   (264)

So far, so good—a sober, restrained speech that acknowledges sexuality but also acknowledges his passage beyond the young affects of

it. Not surely that he is "defunct" in the sense of impotence, but that
at his age "the heyday in the blood is tame," as Hamlet wishfully says
of his mother, "it's humble / And waits upon the judgment" (*Ham.*,
3.4). But judgment in Othello is unusually censorious. Being free and
bounteous to Desdemona's mind seems to require being severe indeed to her body. Her presence in Cyprus, Othello assures the senators, will by no means induce him to scant his military business:

> No, when light-winged toys
> Of feathered Cupid seel with wanton dullness
> My speculative and officed instruments,
> That my disports corrupt and taint my business,
> Let huswives make a skillet of my helm,
> And all indign and base adversities
> Make head against my estimation!

Light-winged toys . . . wanton dullness . . . disports that *corrupt and
taint?* The tone of puritanical disapproval here comes as a distinct
surprise. In Cinthio's novella the Moor is most lovingly anxious to
have his wife accompany him on the journey to Cyprus.[8] Yet Shakespeare's Moor responds as though he were accused of inviting the
whore Bianca with him, so vaguely unclean and nasty seems even
marital sex by comparison to his military occupation. For although
one can discern a "pathological male animus toward sexuality" in
many of Shakespeare's characters,[9] in Othello's case this animus
appears significantly at the point where sexuality comes into potential
conflict with the hero's military "business." Thus the dirtiness of sex
appears to be a product of Othello's need to purify his military
occupation, much as honest wives like Desdemona owe some of their
virtue to dishonest whores like Bianca. The sacred status of an exclusively masculine institution like war is created and preserved by
insulating it from the insidious wiles of women. If war is a positive
means of defining man, woman is a negative means. Men are men,
after all, because they are not women, especially in the case of warriors.

Warriors have traditionally feared that sexual contact vitiates
prowess in the field, and Shakespeare's plays abound in the senti-
ments of Parolles when he urges Bertram to abandon his new-made
wife:

> To the wars, my boy, to the wars!
> He wears his honor in a box unseen

> That hugs his kicky-wicky here at home,
> Spending his manly marrow in her arms,
> Which should sustain the bound and high curvet
> Of Mars' fiery steed. (*AWEW*, 2.4.295)

Manly marrow must be protected at all costs: expend it on kicky-wickies and you will not only lose your masculinity but very likely become somewhat kicky-wicky yourself. The price is too high. For what masculinity, power, stature, and esteem add up to is mana and symbolic immortality. The major source of symbolic immortality is warfare.

Parolles' "To the wars!" and Othello's farewell to the wars testify to the truth of Otto Rank's observation that men care more about their immortality than they do about their lives. Othello's entire speech publicizes the virtues of war, but his comparison of exploding cannons to Jovian thunder—

> And, o you mortal engines, whose rude throats
> The immortal Jove's dread clamors counterfeit,
> Farewell! (3.3.360)

—concisely sums up the principle involved, namely that the closer you get to death the closer you get to immortality. Not immortality after death but before it. An honorable death may send your shade to Valhalla but a heroic life near death can recast your living self in the image of gods. Out of the barrels of war's mortal engines issues the kind of death that cannot touch gods like Jove or heroes like Othello, although it sends lesser men to their graves—which, Falstaff assures Hal, is precisely where lesser men belong:

> Tut, tut; good enough to toss; food for powder, food for powder; they'll fill a pit as well as better. Tush, man, mortal men, mortal men. (*1HIV*, 4.2)

Mortal men like Falstaff's ragamuffins fill pits so that heroic men like Othello can assume Jovian stature by remaining alive.[10] "The moment of survival," Elias Canetti observes, "is the moment of power":

> Horror at the sight of death turns into satisfaction that it is someone else who is dead. The dead man lies on the ground while the survivor stands. It is as though there had been a fight and the one had struck down the other. . . . Whether the survivor is confronted by one dead man or by many, the essence of the situation is that he feels *unique*. . . .

All man's designs on immortality contain something of this
desire for survival. He not only wants to exist for always, but to exist
when others are no longer there. He wants to live longer than everyone else, and to *know* it; and when he is no longer there himself, then
his name must continue.[11]

This casts an explanatory light on Iago's wry response when told by
Emilia and Desdemona that Othello is in a rage:

> Can he be angry? I have seen the cannon
> When it hath blown his ranks into the air,
> And, like the devil, from his very arm
> Puffed his own brother—and is he angry?
> Something of moment then.   (3.4.135)

Iago has it backwards. When immortality is at stake, the puffing of a
brother can be not only endured but profited from; the higher a price
you pay for glory, the more glorious it is.

Brothers' deaths enhance a warrior's greatness, but little
deaths in bed sap his manly marrow, perhaps fatally. He who dies in
bed tonight may die on the field tomorrow. No wonder Othello
assigns the seductive Desdemona to a separate ship for the journey to
Cyprus and dutifully subordinates marriage to warfare. His success is
later implied when he greets his wife in Cyprus with the words "O my
fair warrior!" (2.1.180). Transformed into a kind of Diana-cum-
Hippolyta she is purified both sexually and as it were occupationally.

3. Repletions

By definition, idealism denies the material. Most immediately,
it denies the body. As a stoical idealist, Othello denies or at least
disregards threats to his own body in battle and accepts with equanimity the death of his brother. To deny the body is to deny death,
and vice versa. Thus we see a convergence of Othello's occupation
and his love at the point where the body meets death. This is particularly evident if his greeting to his wife at their reunion on Cyprus
is viewed from the perspective of his farewell to his occupation.

The pun on *occupation* at the end of the farewell speech
prompts a double take. At first glance the speech seems, however
incongruously, a glorification of war; then, at second glance, an
oblique farewell to Desdemona as well, inasmuch as she shares the

values Othello attaches to warfare—pride, pomp, glory, absolute content, a sense of fulfilling immortality experienced at the edge of death. But then we come to the sexual pun in *occupation*, an obscenely anticlimactic end that obliges us to wonder just what Othello has been saying farewell to. Iago replies "Is it possible, my lord?" and with warfare so strongly tainted here by the erotic he might well be asking somewhat confusedly "Do you mean orgasm, my lord?"

Surely not. *Occupation* in the sexual sense is not what the speech depicts but what it nobly outshines. By comparison to the soul-expanding experience Othello describes here, *occupation* is a dirty word, militarily as well as maritally. It labels warfare a trade, a business that pays off in body counts, and marriage the mere rental of a woman's body—precisely what the Moor has sought to transcend. Now both of his loves—the sources of his identity and worth—are simultaneously degraded in his eyes, and his speech records this fall from grace. As the ethereal Desdemona vulgarly corporealizes in his imagination, the glories of war dissolve. What he had thought a marriage was merely a sexual version of a military occupation—a temporary seizure or invasion of property. Alas, entirely too temporary. Already he has been sexually withdrawn and replaced by Cassio—"'tis fit that Cassio have his place," Iago had said not long before, "For, sure, he fills it up with great ability" (3.3.253)—as by order of the Senate he will be militarily withdrawn and replaced by Cassio later.

If we look elsewhere in the play for a correlative to the glories of the farewell speech, we light on Othello's greeting to Desdemona when he arrives in Cyprus. After militarizing Desdemona into "my fair warrior," he goes on to speak of their reunion as if it were the very consummation of their marriage:

> It gives me wonder great as my content
> To see you here before me. O my soul's joy!
> If after every tempest come such calms
> May the winds blow till they have wakened death!
> And let the laboring bark climb hills of seas
> Olympus-high, and duck again as low
> As hell's from heaven! If it were now to die,
> 'Twere now to be most happy; for I fear
> My soul hath her content so absolute
> That not another comfort like to this
> Succeeds in unknown fate. (2.1.181)

Here too, as in the farewell speech, is a moment of emotional repletion associated with death. But this occasion is more complicated.
There, to skirt death's borders in battle and survive generates a sense
of godlike immortality. Similarly here, Othello's escape from death at
sea contributes to the absolute content of his reunion with Desdemona. However, in addition to the relief of survival, the reunion itself
inspires a sense of spiritual fulfillment so intense it borders on death.
Only death can represent and define a perfection so great that desire is
consumed by its own consummation.

This moment of total presence and perfect content is precisely
what Othello grieves for later when he says "Farewell the tranquil
mind! Farewell content!" As his fair warrior, Desdemona combines
the virtues of war with those of love. The reunion spiritualizes the
eroticism thus far lacking in the marriage itself. That is, at this point
the marriage may well be unconsummated, since Othello was called
away from the Sagittary on his wedding night and the couple has been
sequestered from one another at sea since then. Moreover, this same
night they will be roused from bed again by brawling, leaving us
wondering if we are to infer a *coitus interruptus* analogous to the *matri-
monium interruptus* in *All's Well* when the newlywed Bertram aban-
dons Helena for the Tuscan Wars.[12] If so, it would add fuel to a racist
argument featuring an Othello whose nobility only tentatively re-
strains a savage sexuality, now intensified by frustration and ready to
flare into violence.

But this argument flounders against the current of Othello's
stoical idealism, the very nobility with which he is graced and flawed.
For nobility not only builds on frustration, it is defined by it. Without
a world of seductive desires to sacrifice on the altar of temperance, the
stoic is no stoic. Othello, whom the "full Senate / Call[s] all in all
sufficient," almost seems to welcome midnight brawls and, on a
larger scale, Turkish wars. They provide opportunities for him to set
aside the trivialities of private life, to say to the Senate

> I therefore beg it not
> To please the palate of my appetite,
> Nor to comply with heat—the young affects
> In me defunct—and proper satisfaction,
> But to be free and bounteous to her mind.

This Othello is no centaur champing at the sexual bit. If anything, he
is an old warhorse listening for trumpets and, in the interim, feeling
astonished by his luck in love. His reunion with Desdemona is wholly

spiritualized. She is not a wife to bed but a goddess to worship in the temple of neoplatonic love. His rapturously soulful greeting stands out all the more transcendently for trailing the bawdy exchanges of Iago and Desdemona earlier, in which at one point Iago was required to speak of a "black" maid who finds a proper sexual "fit" with a "white [wight]" (2.1.132).

Thus to help account for Othello's explosive passions later on I would propose the frustrations not of a *coitus interruptus* but of a *miles interruptus*. For no sooner has Othello had his marvelous moment of reunion than he discovers that the "wars are done; the Turks are drowned" (202). Happy news there, on the surface of it, yet troubling too, for if the wars are really done, then Othello's occupation's already gone. What will he do for conquests now? Tamburlaine, suffering a similar fate, is driven to contemplate an assault on the gods. Othello is more prudent; he cashes in his winnings from death and warfare and reinvests them in Desdemona and love. From now on his fair warrior is the sole source of that symbolic immortality that once issued from the cannon's mouth.

Unfortunately, this substitution of Desdemona's love for the war he has lost entails a sacrifice, and perhaps a dark portent. Othello's remark to Iago when he first appeared on stage comes to mind:

> For know, Iago,
> But that I love the gentle Desdemona,
> I would not my unhoused free condition
> Put into circumscription and confine
> For the sea's worth. (1.2.24)

Desdemona's virtues may balance the sea's worth, but the reduction of an unhoused free condition to circumscription and confine is as potent with danger as the diversion of pent-up martial energies into a marriage. Othello's later rages issue more from this source, it would seem, than from frustrated sexual desire.[13] Increasingly the lost violence of battle returns to plague a marriage in which Othello's wife has become his enemy.

4. Where's Satisfaction?

If the disappearance of the Turks shifts the center of fulfillment from war to love, Iago's business is to shift it further still, from love to vengeance. But between love and vengeance lies knowledge.

No sooner does Othello deliver his farewell speech than he turns to
Iago and demands

> Villain, be sure thou prove my love a whore!
> Be sure of it. Give me ocular proof,
> Or, by the worth of mine eternal soul,
> Thou hadst been better have been born a dog
> Than answer my waked wrath!   (3.3.365)

For his lost occupation and seemingly lost wife Othello finds a ready
substitute in the desire for certain knowledge, however degrading
and painful. Certainty too is the perfection of desire. To be in doubt is
to be in a state of suspension. It stimulates what Keats might have
called positive capability, an "irritable reaching after fact and reason"
that will put an end to doubt. "Would I were satisfied!" Othello cries
(3.3.395); and Iago slyly explores the ambiguities of *satisfied:*

> I see, sir, you are eaten up with passion.
> I do repent me that I put it to you.
> You would be satisfied?
>
> OTH.   Would? Nay, and I will.

Yes, but how? Through ocular proof? Iago demurs. "It were a te-
dious difficulty, I think, / To bring them to that prospect," to a point
where the Moor may "grossly gape on." "What then?" he asks:
"How then? / What shall I say? Where's satisfaction?" (3.3.405).
    Satisfaction is where it has always been for Othello, in the
mind, not in the body. Desdemona's physical beauty has stood as a
neoplatonic symbol of her inner truth and, by reflection, of his truth
as well. In fact her truth is her troth; it consists in being true to him,
both in the sense of reflecting him truly and of being sexually honest.
Thus it is appropriate that when his suspicions are aroused he demands to be satisfied not sexually but intellectually, as though all his
bodily desires have been spiritually redirected: he lusts for truth. Yet
it seems his lust can be satisfied only by gaping on bodies.
    Curiously, at this point, when Iago is called on to produce
naked bodies in bed, we realize that, materialist though he is, his own
plot rests on a kind of perverted idealism. Floating on lies, detached,
quite literally unsubstantiated, it is as bodiless as Othello's love. That
is what makes it devilish. Because Iago's lies and implications are
divorced from material fact, because they reside only in the jealous
mind, they acquire the sort of remote invulnerability of platonic

Ideas. Like Truth or Beauty, they are abstractions from widespread marital realities—the impure essences of a thousand adulterous occasions, although not one in which Desdemona and Cassio were present. But who can prove that? You cannot prove the existence of either Plato's Ideas or Iago's lies by rummaging in temporal matter.

Lacking visible bodies, then, Iago must make a pretence of satisfying Othello intellectually:

> If imputation and strong circumstances
> Which lead directly to the door of truth
> Will give you satisfaction, you might have it.   (411)

And Othello obliges by momentarily taking up the intellectual gauge: "Give me a living reason she's disloyal."

Shakespeare's stress here falls heavily on the ambiguities of satisfaction. Within a space of twenty lines the word and variants of it appear five times, exposing its sexual meaning—the "proper [personal] satisfaction" Othello denied as his motive for taking Desdemona to Cyprus (1.3.267); its revengeful meaning—the kind of satisfaction the bankrupt Roderigo says he will demand of Iago (4.2.201); and of course its general meaning of completion and fulfillment, with special focus on Othello's being perfectly satisfied that his love's a whore. To be satisfied in this latter way will set the stage for the subsequent satisfactions of violent revenge. But more strangely, to know that Desdemona has been "known"—to have certain knowledge about carnal knowledge—will constitute a kind of perverse sexual gratification as well. If doubt is pain, then absolute knowledge, even of sexual betrayal, is a kind of pleasure.

To provide this pleasure, Iago relies on ocular proof, but of an inward sort; across the Moor's imagination he scribbles the graffiti of adultery:

> I lay with Cassio lately;
> And, being troubled with a raging tooth,
> I could not sleep. There are a kind of men
> So loose of soul that in their sleeps will mutter
> Their affairs. One of this kind is Cassio.
> In sleep I heard him say "Sweet Desdemona,
> Let us be wary, let us hide our loves!"
> And then, sir, would he gripe and wring my hand,
> Cry "O sweet creature!" and then kiss me hard,

> As if he plucked up kisses by the roots
> That grew upon my lips; then laid his leg
> Over my thigh, and sighed, and kissed, and then
> Cried "Cursed fate that gave thee to the Moor!"   (3.3.418)

Though this is hardly satisfying to the Moor, yet it satisfies his perverse desire grossly and violently, as if he had indeed gaped on— "O monstrous! Monstrous!" As a result Iago (as though the ease of it offends his artistic sensibility) is obliged to undo his own work a little: "Nay, this was but his dream" (431), "Yet we see nothing done" (436). Iago is not satisfied, nor does he want Othello to be, even painfully. He is not interested in the satisfactions of certainty, in bringing deferral to a close. He prefers to sustain desire in an infinity of doubt. That alone truly satisfies. Thus when Othello begins to clamor for vengeance, Iago sardonically remarks "Yet be content" (3.3.454)—which is to say, defer the satisfactions of revenge and be satisfied with frustration.

5. Death and Desire

Where's satisfaction now? Othello is persuaded he has found it in a known betrayal:

> Now do I see 'tis true. Look here, Iago,
> All my fond love thus do I blow to heaven.
> 'Tis gone.
> Arise, black vengeance, from the hollow hell!
> Yield up, O love, thy crown and hearted throne
> To tyrannous hate! Swell, bosom, with thy fraught,
> For 'tis of aspics' tongues!

Hieronymo, Titus Andronicus, Hamlet, or Vindice could not have put it better. Satisfaction lies now in vengeance, in "blood, blood, blood" (455), in death. And rightly so. Total fulfillment, Othello said in his reunion speech, verges on death—his own death, the proper climax of his ecstasy. Now, however, certain knowledge that his love's a whore will prove a kind of ecstasy that verges on death too—not his but Desdemona's, an inversion of the little death of love. To know Desdemona sexually is, in the familiar metaphor, to die. To know that Desdemona has been known is not to die but to kill. The violence that should have been expended on the Turks is turned cannonlike on Desdemona and Cassio.

However, to satisfy his desire for certainty, to know that Desdemona has been known, is also a kind of dying for Othello. In the following scene (4.1) he asks Iago what Cassio has told him, and Iago replies

> Faith, that he did—I know not what he did.
>
> OTH. What? What?
>
> IAGO. Lie—
>
> OTH.   With her?
>
> IAGO.   With her, on her, what you will.

To answer Iago's "Where's satisfaction?" we need merely point to Othello at this moment. He is satisfied. He explodes with satisfaction:

> Lie with her? Lie on her? We say lie on her, when they belie her. Lie with her! 'Zounds, that's fulsome.—Handkerchief—confessions—handkerchief— To confess, and be hanged for his labor—first, to be hanged, and then to confess.—I tremble at it. Nature would not invest herself in such shadowing passion without some instruction. It is not words that shakes me thus. Pish! Noses, ears, and lips.—Is it possible?—Confess—handkerchief!—O devil!

And then he falls into a trance brought on by this "shadowing passion."

At this point love and language corporealize together. As Desdemona and Cassio become in Othello's imagination a pair of coupling bodies, and as his own body begins to shake and tremble, so his eloquence splinters into fragments, his meanings are eclipsed by gross significers, and his discourse of reason yields to bodily cries. It is a moment of unrepression or desublimation, or, to call on Plato instead of Freud, it is a moment when Reason sleeps. For then, Plato says,

> the Wild Beast in us, full-fed with meat and drink, becomes rampant and shakes off sleep to go in quest of what will gratify its own instincts. As you know, it will cast off all shame and prudence at such moments and stick at nothing. In phantasy it will not shrink from intercourse with a mother or anyone else, man, god, or brute, or from forbidden food or any deed of blood. It will go to any lengths of shamelessness and folly.[14]

So as Othello's reason descends into a trancelike sleep, the Wild Beast twitches epileptically and awakes to a "shadowing passion." The phrase suggests both a raging response to Desdemona's betrayal and a sensual response reflecting the passion of Cassio lying with or on her—in short, a violent fusion of the emotions of warfare and love. As Othello's imagination creates a shadowy substitute for the sexual act in which Cassio is substituting for him with Desdemona, his emotions reflect Cassio's but also inevitably reflect his own sense of outrage, so that in the climactic collision between sexual and vengeful desires he loses consciousness. The ocular proofs of the imagination prove grotesquely "satisfying" inasmuch as a loss of consciousness is itself a little death.

If Othello's loss of consciousness metaphorically represents the sexual consummation of his shadowing passion, it also represents the climax of his desire to obliterate the images that arouse and oppress him. More than being merely the climactic disintegration of a mind under stress, his epilepsy is also a psychological strategic act. He can erase the imagined act of sex only by erasing imagination itself: his (un)consciousness cries "No!" to its own tormenting products and to the referents they supposedly shadow in reality. In effect his epilepsy is a passive version of his later murder; each annihilates the unbearable.

6. Versions of Obedience

My stress here on the arousal and release of suppressed passions associated with the body is too one-directional; it needs a counteremphasis on the evils of idealism. Othello's violence may require the energies of the body, but its source is the symbolizing consciousness. Thus in the Murder Scene Othello's "cause" is in reality somewhat dingy—merely a desire for personal revenge for the loss of monogamous property seen as an extension of self—but after it has been laundered in noble rationalizations it emerges more bravely as a desire to preserve the purity of the male order ("else she'll betray more men"). Not that male bonding plays a prominent role in Othello's motives—he is no Romeo to Iago's Mercutio, though the parallel has a distant relevance. His bonding is to higher authority, to the Father. First, to God the Father when he converted to Christianity; then to Brabantio, who "lov'd" and "oft invited" him to his house and to whom he filially confided his storied identity; then to the patriarchy of the Senate, who agree to judge the marital case against Othello, as the Duke says, "though our proper son / Stood in [Brabantio's] action" (1.3.71).

The Senate constitutes a grander mirror than Desdemona, and

in the Duke's approving words Othello sees a state-authorized image
of himself that he cannot resist:

> I think this tale would win my daughter too. (1.3.173)
>
> Othello, the fortitude of the place is best known to you; and though
> we have [in Cyprus] a substitute of most allowed sufficiency, yet
> opinion, a sovereign mistress of effects, throws a more safer voice on
> you. (225–28)
>
> And, noble signior,
> If virtue no delighted beauty lack,
> Your son-in-law is far more fair than black. (293)

"I have done the state some service, and they know it," Othello
declares at the end; and, to be sure, he is devoted to the state almost
beyond the requirements of duty. In the Senate Scene, when he
justifies his request that Desdemona be allowed to accompany him to
Cyprus ("I therefore beg it not / To please the palate of my appetite"), he denies sensuality in himself and suppresses it in her. But,
most important in the present connection, he exalts his military
occupation and his devotion to senatorial business. While Desdemona is divorcing herself from her father and wholeheartedly committing herself to him in marriage, Othello publicly and almost
rudely puts her in her place, which is distinctly secondary to the
patriarchal authority of the state and the sacredness of his occupation.

Putting people in their places is one of the things generals do,
or should do, as Ulysses reminds Agammemnon in his famous speech
on the shaking of Degree. As a good general, Othello is conscious of
his place in the state hierarchy, and he is conscious of Desdemona's
place as a woman in a patriarchal society. How ironic then that he
should be involved in two fatal breaches of hierarchy: his appoint-
ment of the "mathematician" Cassio to the lieutenancy instead of the
battle-tested Iago and his wedding of Desdemona against her father's
wishes. The two combine to destroy him. The former breach inspires
Iago to forswear Degree himself and, eliding the difference between
ancient and general, to make a mockery of authority—

> It is as sure as you are Roderigo,
> Were I the Moor, I would not be Iago.
> In following him, I follow but myself—
> Heaven is my judge, not I for love and duty,
> But seeming so, for my peculiar end. (1.1.57–61)

Iago's subversiveness makes good use of Desdemona's. "She did deceive her father, marrying you" (3.3.212). Moreover, for her "not to affect many proposed matches / Of her own clime, complexion, and degree, / Whereto we see in all things nature tends—" (3.3.236–38), and instead to choose a Moor! Unnatural! Yet perhaps strangely natural in a woman sensually given, and what woman is not? Thus Othello is seduced into adopting toward Desdemona and even himself the "natural" perspective of Brabantio the father and a patriarchal white culture. From that standpoint her admirable transcendence of cultural taboos in marrying Othello is transformed into a dangerous return of the repressed, that subversive Venetian subculture in which women's "best conscience / Is not to leave it undone, but keep it unknown" (3.3.209–10).

As we move toward the Murder Scene Othello reaffirms his allegiance to the patriarchal state. When Lodovico hands him a letter with the words "The Duke and the senators of Venice greet you," he replies with rather undue subservience and a curious gesture, "I kiss the instrument of their pleasures" (4.1.217–18). The letter, which "command[s] him home, / Deputing Cassio in his government," so arouses his passions that he strikes Desdemona. Yet while he sarcastically attacks her for her "obedience"—"And she's obedient, as you say, obedient, / Very obedient"—he concludes by saying himself "Sir, I obey the mandate, / And will return to Venice" (4.1.256–61).

Although the state, like Desdemona, has abandoned him for Cassio, yet his obedience to it is as unbending as hers seems pliant. One obedience will punish another. Thus "what erupts in Othello's jealousy," Edward A. Snow shrewdly notes, "is not primitive, barbaric man but the voice of the father, not 'those elements in man that oppose civilized order,' but the outraged voice *of* that order."[15]

7. Occupation and Mystery

Othello's epilepsy may be a kind of little death analogous to sexual orgasm, but this is a figure, and Desdemona does not die figuratively. In fact, as Shakespeare dramatizes it, her murder literalizes the sex-death metaphor.[16] If we have wondered whether the act of marital love has been committed or simply sublimated out of existence, now we have it, the ocular proof that Othello beds his wife. Or, rather, beds a whore. Crying "Down, strumpet!" he throws her on her back and does what he feels is properly if not usually done to strumpets—he smothers her. We do not need Emilia's cry "O who hath done this deed?" to register the presence of sex within the act of violence. In this fatal bedding, we witness a performance of what Tavener's *Proverbs* called "the thynge that is done [that] cannot be undone."

What we see in the Murder Scene is not only an unmetaphoring of the little-death cliché but an enactment of the pun on *occupation* in Othello's farewell speech. The word itself does not appear in this scene, but it has appeared prominently, with a variation, in the Brothel Scene. The Brothel Scene is itself a dramatization of the sexual meaning of *occupy.* There, *occupation* becomes *mystery:* "Your mystery, your mystery," Othello says to the hold-door Emilia (4.2.30) as he pretends to get down to business with Desdemona. His previous occupation of his wife is recalled in terms that stress her role as a "vessel" that should have been preserved "from any other foul unlawful touch" (4.2.83) but, alas, has not:

> The fountain from the which my current runs
> Or else dries up—to be discarded thence!
> Or keep it as a cistern for foul toads
> To knot and gender in!   (59)

The words *whore* and *strumpet* reverberate, and the episode ends with Othello paying for his pleasure by giving coins to Emilia.

In the Murder Scene the focus is on desublimation as Othello enters announcing to his soul his dedication to a "cause" which is noble yet which cannot be repeated in the presence of "chaste stars." The ritual sacrifice he intends and the hieratic style he affects correspond to the idealization of warfare and love in the farewell speech; and the degeneration of this stylized sacrifice to a brutal "murder" (5.2.67) that degrades the act of wedded consummation into the fatal bedding of a "strumpet" corresponds to that speech's fall from martial and marital glories to a crude pun on violence and sex in the word *occupation.* If the Murder Scene is the word *occupation* writ dramatically large, then that word is now occupied by its two most degraded meanings—the warrior's killing business and the strumpet's mystery—both featuring a trade in bodies and each specializing in its peculiar brand of death.

But the kind of death the warrior deals in, and deals out, as part of his occupation prevails over that of the whore. It puts paid to the strumpet's mystery and satisfies eternally. Desdemona has made the rounds, it seems, from Brabantio to Othello (to Cassio, to all male customers, to Othello again), and now at last to Death. Here is perfect content, an end to satisfaction. For Death is a strict moralist in matters of chastity; no wife, however wanton, cheats on him, unless it is with what Hamlet calls My Lady Worm.

To put paid to my own mystery, I should sum up oversimply by saying that in his treatment of Othello's occupation Shakespeare seems to suggest that evil in this play is by no means Iago's private property. It issues from nobility and the received patriarchal values as much and as disastrously as it does from villainy and bestial passion. Anticipating Pascal's remark that "when men seek to become angels they become beasts,"[17] Shakespeare portrays a hero whose heroism achieves its purity by repressing the bestial Iago, by forcing Iago allegorically outside himself to become an independent character. But Iago longs as it were for a reunion, and achieves it in the form of a wedding ("I am your own forever") whose consummation is the death of Desdemona.

That reunion, oddly enough, "perfects" Othello by degrading him to the human condition which it has been his occupation to deny by transcendence. He had thought himself completed when he married Desdemona and took possession of a wife who reflected his inward perfection. But his true completion depends on another form of possession, the demonic, which does not make him demonic but only human. For to be completely human is to be entirely imperfect.

We could put it in terms of puns. I said earlier that the punning *foin* in "occupation" and the *whore* in "abhor" pass unremarked in the play. Similarly, the *hell* in "Othello" also passes unremarked—by Othello himself, by Desdemona, by some critics, certainly by Verdi when he elided it altogether in the title of his *Otello*. Thus when Othello says "Will you, I pray, demand that demi-devil / Why he hath thus ensnared my soul and body" (5.2.309), we make the same mistake as Othello if our gaze falls exclusively on Iago. Even at this point, Othello is too ready to seek the demonic outside himself, forgetting his own words "Now art thou my lieutenant." Moreover, as I emphasized in Chapter 2, Iago is not only Othello's lieutenant, he is Venice's lieutenant, a personification of the hidden veins of misogyny and racism that run in the body politic and bode no good to Venetian wives and black strangers.

To be sure, however, when Othello slays the Turk in himself at the end, he also slays the Christian idealist who once smote a real Turk in what he took to be a noble cause, even as Othello himself smothered the sinful Desdemona in what he took to be a noble cause. Whether Othello conceives of himself as punishing the noble Christian as well as the barbaric infidel, we have leave to doubt, but we can be sure that the playwright who staged the punning deed is most fully aware that noble men and altitudinous causes have worked more base evil on this globe than all the demi-devils and stage villains in Christendom.

Iterance

1. Repetitions

Othello's final speech—with its "Speak of me as I am" followed by "Then must you speak of one . . ."—says in effect "Repeat after me." This means paradoxically that his unique identity is now dependent on repetition—on what Othello himself calls iterance. That is, after Desdemona is dead, Othello tries to bring a halt to Emilia's denunciations by saying "Thy husband knew it all" (5.2.144); but she says blankly "My husband?" and despite his confirmation she repeats "My husband?" twice more until the exasperated Moor finally cries "What needs this iterance, woman? I say thy husband."

Thinking back on the amount of repetition in this play, we too may feel like asking "What needs this iterance?" For no one who has seen or read *Othello* can fail to recall Iago's repeating "Put money in thy purse" six times (plus four variants), or Cassio's wailing "Reputation, reputation, reputation," or Othello's chanting "It is the cause, it is the cause, my soul." Less famously but no less meaningfully are such exchanges as these between Iago and Othello:

> If thou dost love me. . . . You know I love you. . . . I think thou dost. (3.3.120 ff.)

> Utter my thoughts? (3.3.141) . . . A stranger to my thoughts (149) . . . To let you know my thoughts (159) . . . By heaven, I'll know thy thoughts. (167)

> Would I were satisfied! . . . You would be satisfied? Would? Nay, I will! . . . And may; but how? How satisfied, my lord? (3.3.395)

> What? What? . . . Lie— . . . With her? . . . With her, on her; what you will . . . Lie with her? Lie on her? We say lie on her, when they belie her . . . Handkerchief—confessions—handkerchief—To confess . . . Confess—handkerchief! (4.1.33–37)

Othello supplies other examples in addressing Desdemona, then
Lodovico, then Desdemona again:

> Fetch me the handkerchief! My mind misgives.
> The handkerchief!
> The handkerchief!
> The handkerchief!   (3.4.91–98)
>
> Sir, she can turn, and turn, and yet go on
> And turn again; and she can weep, sir, weep;
> And she's obedient, as you say, obedient,
> Very obedient.   (4.1.254–57)
>
> If she come in, she'll sure speak to my wife.
> My wife! My wife! What wife? I have no wife.   (5.2.100)

For that matter the climactic act of the play, the murder itself, has to
be repeated: "Not dead? Not yet quite dead?" (5.2.88).

What then are we to make of all this iterance?

2. *Repetition, Replacement, and Selfsameness*

Identity, the self, the *I:* if these are of major importance in
Othello, then of major importance to them are the concepts of repetition and replacement. Replacement is instrumental from the start. In
the opening lines of the play we discover that from his perspective the
deluded Roderigo has been replaced by Othello as Desdemona's
husband. Therefore, led on by Iago, he intends to replace Othello in
bed. By a similar token, because Cassio has replaced Iago in his
rightful rank as lieutenant, Iago will be revenged by making it appear
that Cassio has replaced Othello with Desdemona.

Iago is the great replacer—in large part because he thinks of
people as pieces on a chessboard to be moved about and "taken."
However they may appear, all humans are alike beneath the skin. Let
them wear their hearts on their sleeves and you will find they are all
wanting creatures—incomplete and imperfect, hence unsatisfied and
full of longing. What they long for is not a lost platonic world of
being, a union with God, or a marriage of true minds, but self-serving
corporeal gratifications. Witness Roderigo itching to do Othello's
duty betwixt his sheets. Witness Cassio eyeing his whore—and perhaps Emilia on the side. For that matter, witness Othello and Desdemona themselves, for it cannot be but she is riggish and he a fortune
hunter, despite all their asinine etherealizing about love.

And if all are alike, then all are exchangeable, Iago included.

Indeed especially Iago, who has already replaced himself when the play begins: "I am not what I am." If you are an actor, as he is, then Honest Iago and Villainous Iago are obverse and reverse of the same coin. On the one side, the pure gold of human concern:

> 'Sblood, but you'll not hear me.
> If ever I did dream of such a matter,
> Abhor me.   (1.1.4)

On the other, a villainous nephew of the old Vice vaunting his rascality on the boards of the Globe. In that generically replaceable role, Iago has succeeded Richard Crookback and will be succeeded in turn by Edmund in *Lear*, although there is certainly a sense in which we acknowledge him as, if not unique, the nonpareil of villainy.

Othello, on the other hand, is irreplaceably himself. If Iago always appears in profile, one side or another of him in eclipse, Othello always appears face-on—three-dimensionally present and accounted for. We catch glimpses of Iago on the turn, caught as it were in mid-exit, whereas Othello always seems to be making an entrance. Iago slips into the play on the coattails of Roderigo's opening lines; Othello comes forth trumpeted by shouts and rumors, blazoned by torches, and demanded by all. Like his parts, title, and perfect soul, he manifests himself truly and always selfsamely in the "I am that I am" tradition, or on the principle enunciated by Feste's old hermit of Prague—"That that is is" (*TN*, 4.2.17).

As the shape of these quotes suggests, such a kind of identity repeats itself, for after all "what is *that* but *that*, and *is* but *is*" and therefore *I* but *I*? So it would seem appropriate that at the beginning of the play Othello repeats himself by retelling his life story and that at the end of it he calls on Lodovico and the others to repeat him by speaking of him as he is. He is hardly unique in this; as I mentioned earlier, everyone is a more than twice-told story. Such retellings recur more often among the aged, no doubt, but we all repeat ourselves—that is how we become ourselves. Identity is not an immutable platonic essence, but it does depend in large degree on our responding predictably on similar occasions. We declare and re-declare ourselves by adhering to principles and maintaining prejudices, by acting in character for fear of violating or losing our sense of who we are. Surely one purpose of a "self"—of repeatable patterns of behavior—is to stabilize us in time, to guarantee that our long-range plans and strategies are not subverted by transient desires or casual inspirations. As the stare of a lion about to charge a kudu must not be distracted by the flight of a bird, so even the histrionic and quick-changing Iago must be steadily repeatably villainous if his plot to bring down Othello is to succeed. But of course it is Othello himself who is the great repeater.

3. *Entropy and the Self*

In the light of information theory, we could regard the self as a message directed to an audience. For a message to contain meaning it must contain difference; and for it to be understood, this difference must be discernible. Entropy—the randomizing of semantic energy—is the measure of the audience's uncertainty about difference. Maximum entropy occurs when there is total uncertainty, when no difference and therefore no meaning can be discerned. When the blood on Macbeth's murderous hands incarnadines the sea, making the "green" one-red, the difference between sea and blood dissolves and nothing signifies. By the same token, when discrete words run indistinguishably together or when irrelevant noise invades and merges with speech, the result is sheer static, a tale told by an idiot.

Maximizing entropy is one way to destroy difference and meaning. Minimizing it, we might argue, is another. Minimum entropy arises from repetition. Normally repetition and redundancy are essential to complex messages because they ward off entropy; redundancy enables us to lose or misunderstand part of a message but to recoup our losses elsewhere in it. Too much repetition and redundancy, however, crowds out information. If a message merely repeats what is already known, then it is devoid of news, and although it may be perfectly comprehensible in itself, the sending of it is pointless. The more predictable it is, the less information it conveys. By the same token, identity—whether that of a jellyfish or a genius—becomes more exact in direct proportion to repeatability of behavior. The Hope diamond is undeniably the Hope diamond because it repeats itself exactly moment by moment, year by year, unless of course we are particle physicists. In the absence of immutable souls, our bodies repeat themselves boringly enough to make us recognizably who we are. Whatever goes on inside us—hopes destroyed, dreams fulfilled, love lost or won—there in the mirror, alas, are the same big ears and noses, the same old scars, the same back of the hand we know like the back of our hand. But of course the most remarkable thing our bodies do is to convert breath into sound, and sound into speech, and speech into accents and rhythms and intonations so stylistically familiar that they announce our identities as reliably as our names do. That is to say, we repeat ourselves. The volatile Pistol is undeniably Pistol because he explodes on every occasion, as Malvolio is Malvolio because he disapproves on every occasion—until he falls in love, and then suddenly, because he is out of character, he becomes news. A little dishonesty—a capacity for departing from habitual patterns of action—may give you a bad press, but it goes a long way toward making you newsworthy. Which is why Falstaff and Iago are more interesting than Hotspur and Othello, and Milton's Satan more interesting than his God.

4. Iterance and Meaning

Honesty overdone, as Iago knows, dies in his own too-much, and petrifies. Consistency kills. A rose is a rose is a rose; and dinosaurs—marvels of consistency—are fossil fuel. There's honesty for you. Similarly, Othello is Othello is Othello, which makes him easy game for an Iago who is not who he is. Othello not only takes pains to remain himself, but he insists on others being absolutely and reductively, not precisely themselves, but what he wants them to be. As Mary Douglas writes, "The yearning for rigidity is in us all. It is part of our human condition to long for hard lines and clear concepts. When we have them we have either to face the fact that some realities elude them, or else blind ourselves to the inadequacy of the concepts."[1] Othello opts for blindness and calls it truth; he demands minimum entropy in others as well as in himself. He will think Iago honest even if he were to clatter about the stage on cloven hoofs. Desdemona will be more than honest, a sexless fair warrior: "With all my heart" (1.3.281). By the time Iago instructs him in the complexities of human nature—

> Who has that breast so pure
> But some uncleanly apprehensions
> Keep leets and law-days and in sessions sit
> With meditations lawful? (3.3.143)

—the point of no return has already been reached. Othello merely replaces a romantic idealization of Desdemona as a saint with a cynical conviction that she is a whore. The streets of his imagination are barricaded with absolutes and stereotypes. Nothing gets through— up to a point.

Thus we seem to have two concepts in collision—repetition and replacement. In Othello's employ, repetition fixes and maintains unique identities. Everyone is alloted his or her self to be kept intact on the Polonius principle of "to thine own self be true"—that is to say, repeat yourself. For Iago, on the other hand, replacement—the substitution of one person for another—elides differences and renders everyone alike. If Cassio replaces Othello in Desdemona's bed, not only do he and Othello repeat one another as customers of the whore but also the irreplaceable Othello merges indistinguishably with a world of cuckolded husbands. By asserting the principle of universal replacement, Iago launches an assault on the privacy of property so dear to Othello. If men can slip with unnoticeable ease into and out of the same situations—or beds—then individual identity dissolves into a common commodity: one half-crown or phallus is as good as another on the Venetian sexual Exchange, and Desdemona's endless turning makes all men alike.

One way Iago destroys Othello's belief in private property is by undermining his monopoly on language, illustrated as we have seen in Act I, where the Moor takes narrative possession of words at the expense of dialogue. In so doing, he threatens both the humanity of others and the nature of drama. For when narrative rules over dialogue too autocratically, as in Seneca for instance, drama is submerged in rhetoric, and monologue usurps the place of plot, action, and the give and take of dialogic speech. Sustained thus, narrative might never end. We should have stories within stories, as we momentarily do. Instead of dramatic interactions, Othello would stand grandly alone on the stage telling the epic story of his life, himself the domineering *I* who reduces everyone else to the status of an inferior *she* or *he*.

But Iago can hardly permit that. Having himself been replaced in the lieutenancy by Cassio, he is not prepared to acknowledge private property for anyone else. To that end, he specializes in iterance. When Othello asks "Is [Cassio] not honest?" Iago replies "Honest, my lord?" and Othello repeats "Honest. Ay, honest?" (3.3.105). A moment later the same pattern recurs when Othello asks "What dost thou think?" Iago replies "Think, my lord?" and Othello repeats "Think, my lord? By heaven, he echoes me" (109).

To echo someone's speech, to repeat his words exactly, is implicitly to affirm that language is public property. Language and meaning could not exist if words were not repeatable and hence held in common. Even Othello's proper name, which refers to him alone,

is not his alone to say; and as though to confirm that fact his name tolls
some thirty-four times in the play (as compared, for instance, to
fifteen for *Lear*). Thus from the time Iago first echoes Othello's
think (3.3.109) to the time Othello roars "By heaven, I'll know thy
thoughts!" (166), the words *think* and *thought* recur some sixteen
times. And the theme of their discourse during this period is meaning, particularly Iago's refusal to divulge his: "What dost thou
mean?"

Othello's demand for Iago's meaning, for what he thinks, is
made futile by its own repetition; the more often the word *think* is
repeated the less meaningful it becomes. That of course is what
happens when any word is repeated often enough; it turns into a kind
of phonic tofu in defiance of the claim by information theorists that
redundancy and repetition guarantee clarity of meaning. To be sure,
when Emilia cries "Villainy!" six times in four lines—

> Villainy, villainy, villainy!
> I think upon it—I think I smell it! O villainy!
> I thought so then—I'll kill myself for grief—
> O villainy, villainy!   (5.2.197)

—we get a pretty clear idea what she means; she means villainy. The
virtue of redundancy is such that five-sixths of her message could be
lost, and she would still make her villainous point. Nevertheless,
what is her point? For in such repetitious abundance, *villainy* makes
us wonder, so that by the time we register its third or fourth appearance, its meaning, which seemed wickedly clear at first utterance, begins to cloud. For instance, is there not an element of *villeiny*,
of "villeinage," in all this villainy? After all, the villain Iago is
Othello's sworn servant ("I am your own forever") as the medieval
villein was bond servant to his lord. Moreover the dead Desdemona
has been a villein too and paid a heavy price for release from her
selfless marital bondage, and even Othello himself is a kind of bond
servant to the state who has just said "Nay, stare not, *masters*. It is
true indeed." Finally Emilia, Iago's marital bond servant, is at this
moment breaking her villeinous bond by denouncing his villainy
(" 'Tis proper I obey him," she says a moment later, "but not now. /
Perchance, Iago, I will ne'er go home"). If to be a villein is to be
villainous in the first three instances, and to forswear villeiny to
denounce villainy, as Emilia does, is also to be villainous, then *villainy*
seems to exhibit some of that whorishly pliant obedience Othello

attributes to the ever-turning Desdemona. Far from confirming its semantic identity, repetition has brought *villainy* to a point where, like Iago, it can announce "I am not what I am."

Looked at one way, then, repetition of the same produces a sense of difference, of not-the-sameness. But that is partly because repetition of the same is, in any strict sense, impossible; in a mutable world, only near-repetition or replacement is possible. When Iago repeats Othello by saying "Honest, my lord?" or "Think, my lord?" he is not so much repeating the words *honest* and *think* as he is replacing them with *"honest"* and *"think."* Setting them within quotes, he converts them into different words, splitting their outward sounds from their inward meanings. As a result they are defamiliarized, made odd and suspect.

It is much the same with Iago's famous "Put money in thy purse." Here is redundance aplenty, which ought to mean clarity aplenty, a message Roderigo and we cannot mistake. And to be sure, "put money in thy purse" means—well, "put money in thy purse." But on repetition, and on such excessive repetition, ghostly quotation marks begin to form around the words, making them at the same time lose meaning and assume an air of disconcerting meaningfulness. Does the phrase have a special Jacobean meaning we don't know of, something technical perhaps, or is it an idiomatic bit of bawdry? Or perhaps Iago is coining his own peculiar metaphor? If so, what is the subject? The phrase interruptively punctuates Iago's running claims that Desdemona and Othello must "change" their sexual favors, he because he is a Moor, she because he is a Moor and old, whereas she is white and young, and a woman. Implications abound. The purse is Roderigo's scrotum or Desdemona's womb. Money and sex are somehow interchangeable. Money breeds, as Shylock reminds us. An empty purse is impotent, a full one virile. To fill a womb is to enrich it. Money passes from purse to purse as sperm does from man to wife, as young wives do from bed to bed, as horns do from husband to husband. Instead of reducing uncertainties about meaning, Iago's redundancies make it multiply like coins in a usurer's purse.

At times Iago functions as an auditory mirror, obliging Othello to hear himself asking questions, exhibiting doubt, and exposing himself as an outsider to the truth. Part of this undermining of his sense of self derives from the undifferentiating effect of echoing, which renders different speech-occasions and different speakers alike. We may even discern a quasi-sexual aspect to this. To make the beast with two backs is to appall property in a bodily way, to destroy the distinctions between the coupling pair. Similarly, in an exchange like the following one, a coupling of speech takes place between Iago and Othello that momentarily dissolves their separateness, if not bodily, then bawdily:

> What? What?
> Lie—
> With her?
> With her, on her; what you will.
> Lie with her? Lie on her? We say lie on her, when they belie
>   her. . . .   (4.1.33)

With Iago's words becoming Othello's words, which in turn become Iago's words, and so on, we may if we have indecent imaginations— that is, if we have imaginations—regard the speeches themselves as making a verbal beast with two backs, shaping in signs a grotesque parody of the property-appalling exchanges of identity when lovers see one another in each other's eyes or exchange the shifters *I* and *thee*. Here, however, Othello takes up not the lover's *I* or *thee* but rather, literally and figuratively, the seducer's *lies*. The two men do not lie together, they *lie* together. At the very least we see Othello's private verbal property passing into Iago's possession and Iago's scurrilities into his own.

The most impressive evidence of this exchange of verbal identity occurs when Iago, seeing Othello approach, suddenly delivers a brief aria in the Moor's own most distinctive style:

> Look where he comes! Not poppy, nor mandragora,
> Nor all the drowsy syrups of the world
> Shall ever medicine thee to that sweet sleep
> Which thou ow'dst yesterday.   (3.3.335)

After this, Iago would be justified in turning to the audience and saying with a smile, "You see, I am not what I am." If he can repeat Othello's style, he can replace Othello himself. After all, what *is* Othello if not a style, a mode of speaking, a story told?

For that matter, Iago can replace Desdemona too—most suggestively when he concocts his tale about sleeping with Cassio:

> I lay with Cassio lately;
> And, being troubled with a raging tooth,
> I could not sleep. There are a kind of men

So loose of soul that in their sleeps will mutter
Their affairs. One of this kind is Cassio.
In sleep I heard him say "Sweet Desdemona,
Let us be wary, let us hide our loves!"
And then, sir, would he gripe and wring my hand,
Cry "O sweet creature!" and then kiss me hard,
As if he plucked up kisses by the roots
That grew upon my lips; then laid his leg
Over my thigh, and sighed, and kissed, and then
Cried "Cursed fate that gave thee to the Moor!"

Here, no identity is certain, and no one irreplaceable. Iago's story itself substitutes for the event it claims to depict; Cassio's dream substitutes for the sexual act with Desdemona; Iago substitutes for Desdemona within the dream; and Cassio substitutes for the Moor.[2] Or, to add a paranoid dimension to it, if Iago really or even playfully suspects Cassio of having cuckolded him in the past, then perhaps the fictional dream replaces a more fundamental scene in Iago's imagination—that of Cassio substituting for Iago with Emilia. In which case Desdemona substitutes for Emilia as Iago galls the Moor with what galls him.

With Iago capable of repeating Othello's words and style and of replacing Desdemona in bed, it is not long before the two characters kneel together and plight their vengeful troth, and not long after that before they say "Now art thou my lieutenant" and "I am your own forever." Iago thus takes the place of Cassio as lieutenant and of Desdemona as pledged partner, and in parasitic fashion the Iago principle substitutes in Othello's heart for his native nobility.[3]

5. The Wanton Handkerchief

The fate of Othello's handkerchief neatly sums up this tendency of the seemingly fixed and irreplaceable to metamorphose into the transient and repeatable. All that remains after Othello and Iago have plighted troth is for Othello to give Iago his mother's handkerchief. But in fact Emilia, and in effect Iago, already has it. Why? To give it to Cassio and deceive the Moor about his wife's fidelity. The fetishistic handkerchief that stands for constancy of love is Othello's most private property; yet it makes the rounds from him to Desdemona to Emilia to Iago to Cassio and at last, as though teleologically,

ιore Bianca. The handkerchief thus proves as transitory as its
ι affections. Even the history of the handkerchief is errant
αιια unfaithful. Othello first says it was given him by his dying
mother, who had got it from an Egyptian charmer who had it of a
sybil (3.4.57–77). After Desdemona's death, however, he says the
handkerchief was "an antique token" given his mother not by an
Egyptian charmer but by his father (5.2.223–24). The changing story
contains a changing meaning as well. In his first account, the magic in
the handkerchief's web enabled his mother to "subdue [his] father /
Entirely to her love," in part presumably because the mummy it was
dyed in came from the hearts of chaste maids (3.4.77). Here the
handkerchief symbolizes paradoxical feminine powers: "chastity em-
balmed has become the means of perpetuating desire" and therefore
of guaranteeing masculine chastity.[4] In the second account, however,
the meaning of the handkerchief is colored by the intervening action.
Calling it a gift from his father to his mother, Othello redefines it as a
masculine talisman to ward off cuckoldry, the loss of which correlates
with Desdemona's supposed betrayals.

If the handkerchief is, as I suggested in Chapter 4, a flag or
sign that in Desdemona's keeping parallels the flag carried in battle by
Othello's ancient, then it is appropriate that when it is lost Desdemona does what Iago usually does—she lies (albeit for redeeming
reasons): "I say, it is not lost" (3.4.87). Losing the sign of chastity,
she plays wanton with words as well and so loses her distinctive truth.
The process is made more apparent when Emilia and later Cassio
insist that "the work" should be "ta'en out" of the handkerchief
(3.3.302). For to "take out the work," as Bianca is asked to do
(4.1.149, 152, 154), is to copy the handkerchief's pattern and thus to
degrade the irreplaceable magic talisman to the status of repeatable
common property.

The whoring of the handkerchief fetishizes the whoring of
Desdemona. In addition, it reflects the fate of her husband. For his
own concluding speech asks that his listeners, those who are to tell his
story, take the work out of his life and render him repeatable. After
all, the real magic in the Moor's web has always been verbal—the
stories of his life that bewitched Brabantio, then Desdemona, and
then the Senate and the Duke. That magic, he hopes, can somehow
be preserved in all its special particularity in the explanatory letters
sent back to Venice. But of course that means entrusting his magic to
narrative repetitions that cannot avoid making it common.

6. The Histrionic Self

I have been tracing the disintegration of Othello's identity, that seemingly indivisible, indelible, platonic self whose heroic essence dissolves under Iago's insinuations and reforms in Othello's imagination in the likeness of the common cuckold.[5] At the end of the play, however, when Emilia confirms Iago's claim not to be what he is, Othello discovers that he too is not what he has seemed, a cuckold, but rather an actor unwittingly playing that role in a comic theatrical staged by Iago. By the same token Desdemona is not a whore but rather The Whore, Cassio not her customer but The Customer, and Iago not an honest, loving, morally indignant friend but The Villain. Moreover, Othello has done his own share of theatricalizing, having cast Desdemona in the part of A Soul Imperiled in the Murder Scene and himself in those of Father Confessor, Judge, and Executioner, when in fact she was simply innocent Desdemona and he, as the dying Emilia said, a "murderous coxcomb."

How much of this does Othello understand? As for his own identity, in his final speech he seems to assume that he has peeled away all false roles so that what remains, for better or worse, is the plain "I am" to be reported truly to the Senate. To his credit, he is aware now of mediation. Between him and the Venetian Senate will be the letters of Lodovico and Gratiano, which can misreport him either mercifully or maliciously. But his "Speak of me as I am" implies that misreports can be forsworn in favor of an honest account of the true Othello. But what is this true Othello? When he himself attempts to deliver such an account to his auditors, what emerges is not the image of a unique and essential self but a series of generic snapshots: The Soldier-Servant ("I have done the state some service"), The Unfortunate Lover ("one that loved not wisely but too well"), The Jealous Avenger ("being wrought, perplexed in the extreme"), then more ambiguously The Unlucky Indian or The Villainous Judean, and finally a fusion of The Infidel Turk and The Venetian Christian. Instead of a core-self discoverable at the center of his being, Othello's "I am" seems a kind of internal repertory company, a "we are."

This view of the self goes back at least as far as Plato's psychodrama acted out by internal rulers, soldiers, and workers. Of course the fact that the self has distinguishable constituents that may conflict, as in a psychomachia, does not mean it is not united. As Alex-

ander Nehamas points out, unity may consist either in coherence or
in numerical identity (singleness), and a lack of the one need not
entail the lack of the other: "The idea that we are faced with conflicting groups of thoughts and desires itself depends on the assumption
that these are the thoughts and desires of a single person: why else
would they be conflicting rather than merely disparate?"6 Even the
multiple personalities of people like Billy Milligan—who exhibits
twenty-four personalities, each distinct in name, accent, and be-
havioral traits7—inhabit one body and are subsumed by one name.

But an expression like "I am playing roles" raises the question
of whether the *I* is something separate from the roles played, as an
actor is. It would seem that the roles the self plays are rather like the
symptoms an emotion evinces; they *are* the self, or at least all we can
find of it. We assume, that is, that our pounding heart, trembling
hands and knees, rising hackles and blood pressure are all products of
an inward entity called *fear*. But if we try to isolate this emotion, it
becomes elusive. Once we have worked our way inward, subtracting
each symptom one by one until all are gone, what then remains that
will answer to the name of *fear?* William James expressed the idea
neatly when he said in effect "I do not see a bear, become afraid, and
therefore run. Rather, I see a bear, run, and therefore am afraid"
(*Principles of Psychology*). Somewhat similarly, subtract the fevered
brow, the coughing, the bloody phlegm, the pain, the lesions in the
lungs, and all the other "symptoms" of tuberculosis and what remains are merely the *Mycobacteria tuberculosis*, which are not the
disease but its cause. Somewhere between its cause and its effects,
tuberculosis itself disappears.

By a similar token, subtract from Othello the grand gesture
and the organ music eloquence, subtract also an audience whose
admiring gaze mirrors back to him an image of The Noble Moor, and
subtract especially Desdemona, now cold as her chastity, and Othello
himself disappears: "That's he that was Othello. Here I am." Thus
it's not surprising that even when he tries to tell the definitive inner
truth about his essential self he is inevitably led outward to the
generically commonplace—The Soldier-Servant, The Unfortunate
Lover, and so on. His final speech gives voice to his earlier claim,
"My parts, my title, and my perfect soul / Shall manifest me rightly"
(1.2.31). But the unique *me* is betrayed by its generic manifestations,
even as the word *parts* turns false and takes on a theatrical cast. That
the self is a series of parts tried on, acted out, and left behind is most

memorably expressed perhaps in Jacques' account of the seven ages of man in *As You Like It* (2.7). Shakespeare implies it also in the mirrorings of Othello. For to see yourself in another, as he does—as we all do in our psychological extensions of Lacan's mirror stage—is to divide as well as to unify the here/thereness of the body/self. As Saussure made us aware, difference is not an embarrassing deviation from a prior normative identity but rather its prerequisite; we *are* by virtue of what we are not, and what-we-are-not is our shadow in a mirror, our parents, our friends, our enemies, and, more pointedly, our imagined selves and our prior selves.

Othello, however, assumes the priority of identity; he is what he so perfectly is. By repeating this identity in words, he acquires Desdemona, who helps to manifest him rightly in Venice. In terms of property, she should be merely ancillary to him, a piece of supplementary goods on the inventory of the self-sufficient capitalist. But as the shaping source of his Venetian identity, she is more than merely property. Insofar as Othello is a reflexive product of her mirrorings, she owns her lord as well as being owned by him.[8] She is, as Michael Neill writes, "the very foundation of his conscious selfhood, the 'place' or citadel of his vulnerable identity."[9]

Or, from another angle, we see Shakespeare reversing the Aristotelean view of woman as incompletely human by having Othello perfect himself by means of her. The diabolical version of this occurs when Othello and Iago pledge their vengeful troth. Othello asserts ownership of Iago when he promotes him—"Now art thou my lieutenant"—but Iago's seemingly agreeable reply—"I am your own forever"—has ominous overtones. Property that is yours forever, that you can't get rid of, in effect owns you. Or rather possesses you, for at this point proprietorship yields to possession, "I own" to "I am possessed (of/by)." The fact that at first Desdemona is *his* wife and Iago *his* ancient and then lieutenant seems to support but actually subverts Othello's belief in the all in all sufficient, fully possessed self.

As we would expect, such a belief has no standing in Iago's scale of values. He dismissed the essential self from the start, from the moment he said "I am not what I am" (1.1.66). Because of this, he becomes, remarkably enough, precisely what Othello thinks him to be, an honest man—the only character in the play who admits that the self is not selfsame. Only a character with histrionic leanings and a sense of comic irony like Iago, or like the grieving self-estranged Hamlet, could make such an admission. Most tragic characters, for instance, lack the reflexive view and hence take themselves far too seriously to believe that they are anything but what they are. They make grand declarations of identity, broadcasting to the gods and lesser humans "Here I am, the all-famous Oedipus" or "This is I, Hamlet, the Dane!" or "Not I; I [Othello] must be found." They call themselves Oedipus, Pentheus, Faustus, Samson, and so on—names graven in marble on Mount Olympus. But Iago calls himself "Iago." He knows that all names, all words for that matter, have invisible quotation marks around them, especially words like *honest* and *truth* and *I*. He knows that to search for the irreducible *I* distinct from all roles is akin to searching for a signified that is not also a signifier.[10] Perhaps that is why he is so elusive and deferentially deferred.

> But when my outward action doth demonstrate
> The native act and figure of my heart
> In compliment extern, 'tis not long after
> But I will wear my heart upon my sleeve
> For daws to peck at. I am not what I am.

Iago is not interested in who he is; he can live without the myth of the *I*. The rest of us are not so hardy. Like Othello, we need to have faith in the roles we play, especially when we are playing ourselves. Otherwise we could never act or speak. We may put ourselves *sous rature*, acknowledging that our self is merely or largely the words and roles that constitute it, but nevertheless in some conditional way, if only as a willing suspension of disbelief, we must believe in the fiction. Without faith in herself *as* herself, as a woman who cannot say *whore* because it abhors her, Desdemona could neither live nor die so honestly. Because she knows she could never play the role of whore, she unselfconsciously adopts the role of chaste and constant wife. She never learns that she is not who she is, but because of that, not despite it, she plays herself wonderfully well.

Othello on the other hand comes to know that he is not who he is. He loses faith in the essential *I* when he loses faith in the essential Desdemona:

> Sir, she can turn, and turn, and yet go on
> And turn again; and she can weep, sir, weep;
> And she's obedient, as you say, obedient,
> Very obedient.—Proceed you in your tears.—
> Concerning this, sir—O well-painted passion!

> I am commanded home.—Get you away;
> I'll send for you anon.   (4.1.254)
>
> I cry you mercy, then.
> I took you for that cunning whore of Venice
> That married with Othello.   (4.2.88)

If Desdemona is the whore who married with Othello, then *wife* is merely a mask she wore. Her real identity is defined by her "mystery," and as her true self takes shape in light of her whorish profession Othello signals his disintegration of self by bidding farewell to his "occupation."

From this time on Othello is an actor attempting to play himself. At the end, knowing that he no longer owns himself, that Iago has taken possession of him as an actor takes possession of a role—"Will you, I pray, demand that demi-devil / Why he hath thus ensnared my soul and body? (5.2.309)—he makes a supreme effort to exorcise the demi-devil and recapture his lost noble identity. If the air of recovered magnificence in his final speech vies with a kind of desperate phoniness, if he is trying to cheer himself up, as Eliot claimed, still he apparently remains unpersuaded by his own rhetoric, like an actor stumbling self-consciously through an old part. The best end for such a performance is a self-imposed silence, even a bloody period.

7. Killing the Turk—Again

That Othello is playing an old part in his final speech is confirmed by the fact that his bloody period represents a climactic instance of repetition. Of course the speech itself culminates a play-long process of repetition beginning when Othello repeats to the Senate the story of his courtly retellings of self to Desdemona and concluding in this final speech where he repeats himself for an audience of Venetians whose charge it is to repeat his story to the Senate. But all of this is verbal repetition—the telling and retelling of the acts of Othello's life—whereas what it leads up to is the repetition of action itself. For in committing suicide the Moor repeats in a different context his killing of a malignant Turk, in Aleppo once. Let me pursue this matter of rekilling the Turk on a wider scale, using it as a crowning instance of the role of repetition in Othello.

Repetition, as I've said, is Othello's natural mode—and properly so for a platonist: if the eternal is impossible in a world that runs on time, repetition is the next best thing. If the platonic truth is an immutable origin, it cannot be gained by going forward as toward a Utopia in the future, but only regained by repetition—hence Plato's association of truth with recollection (*anamnesis*), and hence archaic man's employment of ritual repetition to abolish time and recapture the sacred past, *in illo tempore*.[11] Repetition wards off change and the corruptive ills of time. "The elementary living entity," Freud remarks, "would from its very beginning have had no wish to change; if conditions remained the same, it would do no more than constantly repeat the same course of life."[12] This leads Freud to argue that repetition is a kind of conservatism gone mad, not merely a refusal to change but an instinctual return to pre-life, to death. Whatever one thinks of the death instinct, it is surely the case that to be too true to your past self may inhibit adaptation and either seal you up in time catatonically or conduct you directly to extinction.

That this concept of truth as repetition of the selfsame is itself in doubt is implied when Othello is driven mad by the supposed fact that Desdemona "can turn, and turn, and yet go on / And turn again" (4.1.254). If turning is equivalent to error, then Desdemona is untrue to her husband; but if repetition is equivalent to truth, then she is true to herself by virtue of her repeated turnings. Thus she is either immutably false or truly mutable.

But of course this turning Desdemona exists only in Othello's duped imagination. Yet a similar paradox is suggested if we consider the real Desdemona, she who seems almost constitutionally unable to do anything but repeat herself. The more Othello changes, the more blindly devoted and inhumanly constant she becomes. Thus she is most true to him and to herself at the moment when she forswears the truth and lies about who killed her—"No one; I myself." In a double sense Desdemona is too good to be true.

Defining truth in terms of temporal repetition is analogous to defining it in terms of spatial unity, since both aggrandize selfsameness. Certainly unity ranks high in Othello's scale of values. His dedication to the unified self derives from two directions, the Christian and the military. That Christianity is the religion of oneness needs no documentation; it prided itself for imposing the rule of unity on polytheistic paganism—on the kind of paganism perhaps from which the once-barbaric Othello has converted. Nor is the soldier's devotion to unity surprising; armies may be marked by hierarchical differences—by Degree, as Ulysses so famously proclaims in *Troilus and Cressida*—but all those differences exist to guarantee unity of command, thus imitating the great chain of being which descends from and reascends to the one divine commander.

Christianity and the military, and sometimes both at the same time, are preoccupied with imposing order and unity, which means dispelling heresy and enemies. Thus as Christian general, Othello's business is to cry "Keep up your bright swords" in the streets of Venice, to rescue Cyprus from Turkish aggression, to put an end to drunken brawls, to quell insurrection within his own marriage, and, when the truth is known, to do away with the devilish Iago, if he can, and eventually with himself. Thus if we key on Othello's final lines—

> And say besides, that in Aleppo once,
> Where a malignant and a turbaned Turk
> Beat a Venetian and traduced the state,
> I took by the throat the circumcised dog,
> And smote him, thus.

—then we might take one main line of action in the play to be the militant Christian's quest for the Turk.

This questing action has a kind of allegorical doubleness, inasmuch as it equates the actual Turks with the Turk in *Othello*. For instance, in the opening scene the rumors in street and Senate focus first on the activities of Othello and Desdemona and then on those of the Turkish fleet. The implication is that Othello's apparent seizure of the Venetian magnifico's property reflects the Turks' intended theft of Venetian Cyprus. This is a perfectly conventional view inasmuch as Moors were, as foreign infidels, virtually equivalent to Turks: "The word 'Moor' was very vague ethnographically, and very often seems to have meant little more than 'black-skinned outsider,' but it was not vague in its antithetical relationship to the European norm of the civilized white Christian."[13]

Yet it is this particular Christianized Moor who is called on to rescue Cyprus from the Turks, and hence to do what that Christian hero Don John of Austria had done in 1571 when he led the fleet of the Holy League, composed of many Venetian vessels (and one Spaniard named Cervantes), against the Turks and won a spectacular victory at Lepanto. When Othello's marriage is officially sanctioned, he is declared "far more fair than black" and his identity as Venice's Christian savior seems confirmed. Yet, as I suggested in Chapter 2, some pitchy residue of Iago's accusations and our own early uncertainty remains. The image we had of the Turkish raider who in a sense "beat a Venetian and traduced the state" by defeating Brabantio and making off with Desdemona—was it a gross lie or a disconcerting half-truth that has been repressed and sublimated under pressure of state business? If Desdemona has seen through Othello's black face to his true inner countenance, perhaps Iago has seen through the whitewash of Othello's religious conversion to the heathen darkness beneath, has glimpsed the Turk within the Christian.

In any event these signs of Turkishness in the Christian warrior are given added force when the storm destroys the enemy fleet. At this point it appears that the play has been purged of Turks, making way for love's blissful reunions. But then dissension returns in the form of Cassio's brawl, at which point Othello exclaims—

> Are we turned Turks, and to ourselves do that
> Which heaven hath forbid the Ottomites?
> For Christian shame, put by this barbarous brawl!   (2.3.164)

So it seems the Turks are not dead after all, only relocated rather ominously within the Christian community. Unable to invade Cyprus one way, the Ottomites have done so another, this time led by Othello's own lieutenant, who is in turn led by his ancient.

By now it is evident that barbarity recognizes no boundaries. If it seemed present but suppressed in Othello earlier, so was it apparently in the proper Cassio. Where it is not suppressed in the least of course is in Iago, except for tactical purposes. Thus for the Turk to subdue the Christian in Othello requires merely a few restrained hints and tactful silences by his honest ensign. These lead to a licensing of Iago—"Now art thou my lieutenant"—that quietly marks the ascendancy of violence in the Moor. From this time on the answer to his own question—"Are we turned Turks, and to ourselves do that / Which heaven hath forbid the Ottomites?"—is a repeated Yes.

In the Murder Scene Othello attempts to play the role of Christian priest by calling on Desdemona to repeat her sins, and hence to abolish time and drive out the alien evil. He suppresses the Turk in himself in an effort to exorcise the Turk he imagines lurking in his wife's soul. But when she refuses to play her part by confessing her sins, his role collapses into barbarism as he is forced to call what he intends to do a murder instead of a sacrifice. If she will not repeat her sins, he will repeat his "virtues," which derive from his repeated willingness to dispense with evil by murder. After all, generals specialize in murder, though not usually on such a modest scale, and if they can murder often enough, their reward is to live in a world purged of dissension, where all is as they would have it—one.

Which gets us back to unity and repetition and their fusion in Othello's suicide. When he kills himself Othello repeats an act of violence committed in Aleppo once, a purificatory act whereby Christian unity was enhanced through the elimination of a barbaric Turk. This conquest of the divisive outsider is repeated psychomachically when Othello the Christian does away with Othello the Turk.

However, at this point Shakespeare and Othello divide company. For Othello unity is all. In Aleppo he was completely Christian and all Turks were outside him. Now, in his private version of the ritual return to what took place *ab origine,* he calls on repetition to abolish time and recapture lost innocence. But Shakespeare will not have it so simply.[14] The price of truth conceived of as a perfect unity preserved by repetition is nothing less than death. To kill the Turk for the sake of Christian unity, you must also kill the Christian. For the two are one, at least bodily, and the dagger that pierces the infidel takes a lethal toll of Christian blood.

Thus Othello reverts at the end to the same unifying/repeating mode that has characterized him from the beginning. In this final exemplification of it, his passion for unity and repetitive selfsameness is seen to be not self-creative but self-destructive. The source of evil in this play is not merely Iago, the enemy of purity and order, but Othello, the enemy of division and change. Through repetition Othello wants forcibly to reaffirm his fixed truth and nullify what he takes to be the sources of evil—time and mutability. Yet in doing so he merely illustrates the fact that truth wedded to itself remains true only in the tautological style of Feste's old hermit—"That that is is." Seeking to preserve meaning by petrification, Othello falls prey to time's turnings, in the form of Iago, and turns and turns again until at last he turns on himself. Even more devoted to the selfsame than he, Desdemona does not turn in the least when her world begins to revolve violently about her. She repeats her single truth faithfully, endlessly, at times maddeningly, and goes to her grave as if on rails.

As for Iago, the consummate actor, he can repeat Othello and replace Desdemona, can be all things at all times, but finds in the midst of these shifts and turns that to be too busy is some danger.

Pinned down at last like Proteus and called upon by Othello to dispel confusion by telling a true story, he sardonically takes the hermit of Prague's line, replying in a parody of Othello's own repetitive mode— "What you know, you know"—while declaring in his own style that he will repeat nothing—"From this time forth I never will speak word."

Iago's refusal to repeat himself at this point means that Othello's story cannot be fully told, that the causes and motives that underlie its plot remain in Iago's diabolic possession. His silence forces us to wonder about the fate of Shakespeare's play. If Othello's story is also Shakespeare's story, then private property seems to vie with theatrical property under the entrepreneurial supervision of Iago. That, however, is a subject that deserves a chapter to itself.

The Properties of the Play

1. Iago and Inbetweenness

Since at least 1817, when Hazlitt called Iago "an amateur of tragedy in real life," critics have remarked on the theatrical artistry of Othello's ancient.[1] Stanley Edgar Hyman makes the most concentrated case, picking up on Bradley's claim that "Shakespeare put a good deal of himself into Iago" and arguing that "for Shakespeare, Iago is a merciless self-portrait as artist-criminal . . . and a therapeutic symbolic action of purging away the guilt of Shakespeare's Faustian craft."[2] What this means in Hyman's subsequent discussion is that Iago mimics the playwright's craft in staging scenes and manipulating people, in creating illusions, in improvising to meet occasions, and in exhibiting a full repertory of lies ranging from the "flat untruth" to the "artistic suggestion-in-non-suggestion."

Cataloging Iago's stage practices is less meaningful, however, than registering their staginess. In the tradition of the theatrical villain he takes a showy pleasure in sharing with the audience his knavery, his many motives, his manipulative cleverness, even the labor pains of his creative plotting—"How, how?—Let's see" (1.3.395). By staginess, then, I mean mediation. Situated between two idealists, Othello and Desdemona, who believe they communicate not *in* but through words and bodies—that is, who think signs and referents (and signifiers and signifieds) are so fast married that communication is virtually intuitive—Iago stands for mediation, for inbetweenness and the shaped made-up-ness of things.

The logocentric assumption of Othello and Desdemona that signifiers and signifieds are covertly married is emblematized by their own covert marriage, by the fact that they themselves appear on stage as husband and wife sans signifier—without any declarative ceremony. On the other hand, when Iago "marries" Othello at the end of Act 3, Scene 3, he insists on ceremony:

Do not rise yet.
[*Kneels*] Witness, you ever-burning lights above,
You elements that clip us round about,
Witness that here Iago doth give up
The execution of his wit, hands, heart,
To wronged Othello's service! Let him command,
And to obey shall be in me remorse,
What bloody business ever.   [*They rise.*]

Although much of his insidious wooing is accomplished without
words, relying on the suspiciousness of silence, when it comes to
murder, Iago, like a bride marrying above her rank, is especially
anxious to seal his good fortune in ritual. Or, rather, in a parody of
ritual, for his business is to subvert mediation in all its forms, to set
down the pegs that make not merely music but traditional ceremonies, honest words, gestures, facial expressions—signs, in short.
Indeed *en*-signs.
    As I mentioned in Chapter 4 it is no accident that Iago is
Othello's ancient or ensign, his flag-carrier. He himself makes a point
of it as he prepares to leave the streets and join the Moor:

Though I do hate him as I do hell-pains,
Yet for necessity of present life,
I must show out a flag and sign of love,
Which is indeed but sign. That you shall surely find him,
Lead to the Sagittary the raised search,
And there I will be with him.   (1.1.156)

Iago's stress on signs here draws attention to mediation, to signs as
signs, to false signs that are indeed "but signs"—those in which the
shadow of evil intent falls *between* sign and referent to fashion a lie, as
Iago's shadow will fall between Othello and the truth of Desdemona
to fashion a murder. It draws attention also to the centaurian sign of
the Sagittary which shows out a flag of barbarism, which is indeed but
sign, before the inn where the Moor and his bride are presumably
attempting to consummate a marriage.
    But Iago's inbetweenness is manifested not only within the
play, in Venice. His puns on his emblematic military rank also get in
between the audience and the Bradley-like illusion of Iago the Venetian. He is literally, he reminds us, a flag or sign of a man—in short, a
character, not a person.
    Or, rather, he is a metacharacter. As such, he undoes what is

usually regarded as the business of the actor: to create a convincing illusion of reality by converting dialogue into speech, script into natural behavior. Instead, Iago turns his own seemingly impromptu speech back into dialogue and script, into the stuff of the stage. For him to say "I am not what I am" (1.1.66) and swear "by Janus" (1.2.33) is appropriate not merely because his Janus-like profile reveals knavery to us in the Globe while exhibiting "honesty" to his fellows in Venice but also because it reveals artifice to us and "reality" to them. As a walking lie he emblematizes the pervasive doubleness of Shakespeare's task, simultaneously to make and match: to make a play that matches life.

Iago's soliloquies illustrate this perfectly. In them he at once muses silently in Venice and speaks publicly in the Globe. Insofar as soliloquy is a means of suggesting depth and inwardness of character, his soliloquies lend him a certain substance as a real "person" in Venice, the only person with an articulate inner life; but insofar as soliloquy is a device to keep an audience informed, they sabotage his reality and declare him an artificial stage figure, a nephew of the old Vice, the only character who knows and unabashedly admits he is a character in a play—hence, a metacharacter. When Iago comes forward to address the audience in soliloquy, he denies his equality with the other characters. He strides into the mirror of art, only to pause half-in half-out and assert both his metadramatic discreteness from the realities of Venice and his illusionistic discreteness from the realities of London. This violation of the realistic "rules" of the play observed by the other characters on stage is a theatrical equivalent to his violation of the communal mores observed by other "people" in Venice.[3] To him, rules, norms, and principles, wherever they exist, are items of blind faith to which he issues a devilish *non serviam*. Only fools like Othello have such faith, and they pay dearly for it.[4]

Iago's doubleness is in the Freudian sense uncanny—the familiar given an eerie turn. For doubleness on stage is familiar enough. As Bert O. States points out, the actor never quite fully invests his role:

> He is always slightly quoting his character. . . . No matter how he acts, there is always the ghost of a self in his performance (not to be confused with egotism). Even the most unsophisticated theatergoer can detect something else in the characterization, a superconsciousness that could be nothing other than the actor's awareness of his own self-sufficiency as he moves between the contradictory zones of the illusory and the real, *vraisemblance* and *vrai*, seeming and being. . . .[5]

I wonder, however, if Iago may not invert this slight divestiture. In his case, is it not the character rather than the actor who is the ghost, so that instead of an actor quoting Iago's lines we have Iago speaking his own lines through the voice of the actor? In other words, does Iago the demonic character take parasitic possession of the actor who plays him? Well, of course that's fanciful. But surely not unactable. To gain such an impression, the actor would have to play not just Iago but himself as well—himself in the role of an actor possessed by a character, compelled at times almost against his will, somewhat puppetlike, to say what he says and do what he does. At the end of Act 3, Scene 3, when Iago says to Othello "I am your own forever," the diabolic spirit would pass like ectoplasm from the actor playing Iago to him who plays Othello. Thus exorcised, the actor would now be free to play his role as Iago like everyone else, and Iago would return to being merely a character. Now it is Othello who becomes possessed and driven by an alien spirit, who turns Janus-faced and double, who in his worst moments—say, in the dialogue leading up to his epilepsy— finds his voice uncannily taking on the accents of Iago.

In any event, just as Iago gets in between and destroys the marriage of Othello and Desdemona, so he gets in between and deconstructs the audience's theatrical marriage to the illusion of reality in Venice. As a johannes factotum of the theater himself— actor, director, playwright, prompter—Iago is the antithesis of realism. Of course as a tempter to evil he relies on the realistic appearance of honesty, and philosophically his view of the world is crudely realistic. Metadramatically, however, he makes it clear that the emperor of Realism is clothed in highly visible quotation marks when he is around. Without him, we would religiously indulge our Coleridgean poetic faith, our natural talent for seeing through signs and suspending disbelief. Taking a cue from the idealistic Othello and Desdemona, we might well assume that our epistemological marriage to the events in Venice were made in heaven, not fashioned by vulgar theatrical ceremonies on the boards of the Globe. But Iago intervenes—the impediment to the marriage of true minds in the theater as well as in Venice. Instead of saying "the perfect ceremony of love's rite," which is the poet's proper function (Sonnet 23), Iago the poet *manqué* substitutes an imperfect ceremony, a black mass parody of a wedding in which he takes Desdemona's place and speaks fair words with devilish meanings. Had Desdemona played the interior playwright, surely we should have had a true troth plighted betwixt us and the depicted world. But in between us and the light of her truth appears Iago, to cast the shadow of a lie across Shakespeare's stage. Not that Shakespeare is defining his craft as a lie. Rather, I should think, he is defining it in this case as a tragedy. To say "the perfect ceremony of love's rite" is the proper function of the comic rather than the tragic poet, and in that role Shakespeare does more than his share of haling young lovers before the altar of his hymeneal art. The perfect ceremony of tragedy, however, is not a wedding but a killing, and as a participant in that ceremony Iago is functional in the extreme: Shakespeare wields him like a ritual knife in an action that drives straight to the heart. Thus in creating Iago, Shakespeare had no need to purge himself of the "guilt of his Faustian craft," as Hyman suggests. His craft is the tragic craft; it calls for Iago to do as he murderously does and for Shakespeare to write as he murderously writes. It is no sin for a man to labor in his vocation.

2. Iago's Motives

Because Iago is functional in the extreme, so is Shakespeare's plot. Anyone talking about *Othello* is almost obliged to say "The plot is superbly constructed, with virtually every element skillfully exploited by Iago so as to hasten the final catastrophe."[6] But although everyone agrees the plot is well motivated, few agree about how well motivated Iago is. Hence an entire book by Hyman titled *Iago: Some Approaches to the Illusion of His Motivation.*

Hyman explains his lengthy subtitle by putting as much distance as he can between himself and Bradley. "Let me say this as firmly as possible: as a character in a play, not a person, Iago has no motivation. His entire existence consists of words on a page: he has no psychology, no character or personality, no history (he had no past before the play began, and has no future after it ends)" (pp. 4–5). Rudely exposed like this, stripped bare of mimetic reality, Iago can only clutch at fig leaves of motivation offered him by a playwright who would a little o'erstep the immodesty of nature. Shakespeare, that is, "must create the illusion (again by means of words on the page) that such a figure as Iago is motivated in everything that he does" (pp. 5–6).

One problem with this otherwise admirable proclamation is that it endows motivation with an illusionary status no more peculiar to it than to anything else in the theater. When speech comes from a script and clothing from a costume box, when faces are painted, actions rehearsed, and scenes set, what makes motivation so particular? By this exacting criterion, to write about any theatrical matter would require our saying "Some Approaches to the Illusion of [Speech, Action, Scene, Clothing, etc.]." In fact Hyman should have titled his own book not *Iago* but *The Illusion of Iago*, because like everything else in the play Iago is, as he admits, not what he is.

In short, we are talking about a play. Which is entirely acceptable to Iago. That is, to label anything about him an illusion is rather redundant when that is precisely what he himself, honest in duplicity, repeatedly does. Othello and Desdemona are riveted to their realistic identities; they would be appalled to discover not only that they are in a theater as well as in Venice but also that they are not in fact Othello and Desdemona but Richard Burbage and a boy actor (and married to boot!). Iago, however, freely acknowledges what he both is and is not, and revels in his revelry. Thus he is signlike both in the Saussurian sense that attributes meaning to what a sign is not and in the Derridean sense of what a sign is not yet. He is the very non-essence of semantic deferral; no matter how much he tells us about himself and his motives we never feel we have come to an end-stopped truth. Meaning is never identical with itself, and neither is Iago. His being consists in not-being, his meaning in what is not meant.

In this light, then, the question Coleridge posed in his famous phrase "the motive-hunting of motiveless malignity" is actually "Is the illusion of Iago's motivation illusory?" Does Iago protest too much? Is he really fuming with indignation because he was passed over for the lieutenancy? Is he consumed with a desire for vengeance because he suspects Othello and Cassio of bedding his wife? Perhaps, perhaps not.[7] The actor must decide, as he must also decide whether to play Iago—or to be played by Iago—as a latent homosexual, a xenophobic racist, a sadist, a misogynist, a satanic demi-devil, a Machiavellian misanthrope, and so forth.[8] Obviously no one can bring all of these Iagos on stage in one performance. But whichever one(s) the actor chooses to play, he will be false to his role if he fails to incorporate into his performance something of Iago the artist.

One tangential virtue of Coleridge's famous phrase is its suggestion that in the character of Iago Shakespeare has demystified the concept of motivation. Insofar as motivation is held to be originary and inward, at the source of things, it is normally taken to be more real than the behavior it produces—especially when *real* is defined as "originary and inward, close to the source of things." However, if Iago is indeed motive hunting, then motivation is not the source of his behavior but merely another form of it, as fictional as his lies. In that case we are obliged to search for the motives for his motive hunting, a search that takes us backward like a crab into an infinite regress. Since we can always find something prior to a point of origin—the chaos before Creation or another universe in which our Big Bang was a black hole—we must at some point cry out like Aristotle "Enough!" and posit an Unmoved Mover. In *Othello* or any other Shakespearean play the likeliest candidate for Unmoved Mover is the elusive playwright from Stratford, if only because our ignorance of *his* motives is more infinite than any regress. Thus there is no better place to cry "Enough!" than the point at which a search for Iago's motives becomes a search for Shakespeare's motives.

At the same time, however, an attempted transition from Iago to Shakespeare is instructive, because at that point a merger of motives does take place in what might be called, if not motiveless malignity, something rather similar and nearly as sinister—aesthetic disinterestedness. For the one motive we can safely attribute to Shakespeare is the desire to write a good play—a good murderous tragedy that will strew the stage with bodies and bring the audience's collective heart into its constricted throat. Thus his own malignity toward his characters, his blithe willingness to subject them to anguish and agony, is, monstrous as it sounds, aesthetically motivated. Which is to say that it is not malignantly motivated at all, because far from bearing ill will toward Othello and Desdemona, Shakespeare must surely be delighted with the Moor and his bride, even as the one smothers the other. Contemplating them with one auspicious and one dropping eye, he must murmur

> How sad, how sorry, how brutal—but how marvelously right! That villain Iago wrought well. Now, let me revive Desdemona just for an instant—it will pump a little hope into the audience—then smother her again. A final gasping moment of struggle and terror, then death. There, that's it, perfect! Anne, Anne, where are you? Listen to this. . . .

And, to be sure, Iago must be sitting somewhere too, smitten with awe and wonder, thinking "Ah, that villain Shakespeare, what a clever dog! To be sure, I was not bad myself—aesthetically, that is. We do make a fine team. Now, if he will just get me out of this play alive, like Falstaff, perhaps we can do something else—*King Lear*, for instance—I could play Edmund. . . ."

So I suggest that Iago's "motives" can be attributed less to Iago the man (the illusion of a man with motives) than to Iago the artist, the shadow of Shakespeare the artist, with whom he shares a total absence of malignant intent, whatever he says, and a maximum interest in doing whatever it takes to maneuver this play to its gratifying tragic conclusion.

Of course I exaggerate the role of artifice in Shakespeare's art. Desdemona's terror and Othello's anguish in the deathbed scene issue not from a self-conscious preoccupation with dramaturgical technique but from a sympathetic imagination in which human feeling flows into artful feeling with, by this time in Shakespeare's career, scarcely a ripple of resistance. Still, even if they are resolved as if by second nature, artful considerations are inevitably present. Subtract all human feeling and they alone remain, in the shape of a character called Iago.

Let me take this a bit further by returning to the efficiency of Shakespeare's tragic plot and to Iago as master plotter. That Iago is a plotter goes without saying. He revels in plots, sees them everywhere—suspects Othello of wearing his nightcap, suspects, now that he thinks of it, Cassio of lusting for it too, and may even be casting mock-suspicious glances at handsome nobles in the boxes as he says all this. When he is not suspecting plots in others, he is inventing them himself. The opening words of the play catch him in midplot, or in midplots, for to accomplish one plot (making his fool his purse) he has been pretending to be busy with another one (bribing Desdemona into Roderigo's bed). In this respect too he resembles Shakespeare, who, not content with the one plot he inherited from Cinthio, has conjured Roderigo out of thin air and thrust him on stage so Iago will have someone to practice on before he turns his attentions to Othello.

Roderigo is an addition to Cinthio's plot; his presence multiplies plots and emphasizes the superfluous in Shakespeare's art, the superfluous that largely constitutes his art. Superfluous because the Iago-Roderigo plot functions as an analog to the Iago-Othello plot, and analogs are superfluous where plot is concerned. In the evolving action, analogs do not add or subtract, multiply or divide; they are an "equals" sign that goes nowhere, a form of doubling that defers the causal thrust, much as the artful ornamentation of a sword is superfluous and if carried too far may prove a hindrance to its cutting action. Iago and Shakespeare both take an interest in plotting that exceeds the needs of their own master plot—Iago because he enjoys plotting for plotting's sake, Shakespeare because his dramatic craft does not live by plot alone but presupposes doublings, recursions, correspondences, symmetries—a making of patterns as well as a shaping of clean efficient actions.

Still, let us focus on efficient actions, on plots that are, as Aristotle said they should be, causative and well motivated. Unfortunately, however, *cause* and *motive* are Janus-faced concepts. On the one hand they refer to points of origin the pursuit of which leads into infinite regresses. Iago himself is no introspective hunter of origins. (He trots out his motives and causes quickly, mounts himself and his plot on them, and gallops off with never a backward glance. Even at the end of the play when he is given a grand opportunity to justify and/or to brag about his villainies, he locks himself in silence: "What you know, you know." Is he being secretive to vex his audience? Is he overcome by the enormity of his deeds? Or is he unable to answer because he knows no more than they why he has done as he has done? In any case, the motives have disappeared, as though for him and Shakespeare they served their purpose, made a beginning, and there's an end on it.

On the other hand, they may have made their beginning because of their end, for causes and motives are ends as well as beginnings. A motive is within the agent before he acts, generating his action, but it is also the projected result of that action. To the question "Why?" that hangs in the air at the end of the play, Iago might have replied "Because I had grievances, suspicions, hatreds" or, equally logically, "To destroy his marriage." Similarly, the cause in Othello's "It is the cause" is both the driving force that initiates his murder of Desdemona—his indignation at her supposed betrayal— and the terminal effect aimed at—his desire to prevent her from betraying more men. Moreover, as one would expect from Othello, the cause is hierarchical as well as temporal—there is the low degrading sexual cause that must not be revealed to the chaste stars and the transcendent "altruistic" cause of preserving the honor of other men.

Looked at this way, a cause may itself be the result of a cause— not a prior cause but a subsequent one. The end—Aristotle's final or telic cause—may as it were precede and precipitate the beginning, or efficient cause, to bring about an aesthetic form.[9] This is especially true in tragedies, because although the gestating playwright may not yet know where his play will take place, who his hero will be, or how his plot will develop, he does know precisely how everything will end—in death. The hero will die. Moreover, he will die because of something he himself does, because of an act triggered by *hamartia*. Why does he perform this act? "Because he must die" is as proper an answer as "Because of a tragic flaw within him." Whatever the latter may be, whatever the playwright chooses it to be—hubris, impulsiveness, jealousy, ambition, nobleness grown to a pleurisy—it will be an aesthetic product of his future death: the beginning of a plot must be pregnant with its own end. Here again, Iago's motives are aesthetically rather than realistically motivated. Their excessive number—his nonpromotion, his love for Desdemona, his various fears of cuckoldry—calls such extravagant attention to motivation as to demystify it. Iago seems to be saying "I am about to do terrible things. I must have reasons. What could they be?"—very much as Shakespeare seems to be saying "I am going to have Iago do terrible things. He must have reasons. What could they be?" (The nearest analog to this seems to me the demystification of the classical unity of time, and the exposition it entails, by Prospero and Miranda in Act 2, Scene 1 of *The Tempest*.) In any event, a play with an ending fraught with so much pity and fear requires a well-motivated plot and plotter, a plot whose causal design depends on villainous designs.

Design, with its semantic three-way stretch, is a word tailor-made for Iago; it fits him as "motive or aim," as "pattern," and, in hyphenated form (*de-sign*), as "de-meaning." In true Iago style, these various senses of the word efface one another. For example, aesthetic design (design as "pattern") suppresses signs as symbols of meaning by foregrounding formal elements such as congruence, symmetry, and recurrence. Meaning yields to geometry. Thus Iago "de-signs" or demeans signs not only when he divests words of meaning by lying but also when he transforms meaningful humans into causal elements or phases of his plot. For causation converts integral ends into opportunistic means. Cassio must be gotten drunk so he will provoke a riot so he will be cashiered so he will solicit Desdemona for reinstatement so Othello will grow suspicious and, after a few more *so*'s, kill his wife. At each point a person is reduced to a function, and his or her action is stripped of its nuances of human feeling and meaning in order to become a link in a causal chain. If *B* advances the plot from *A* to *C*, it has done its job and can retire unlamented. Plotting and causation dehumanize in the interests of a design that can be achieved only by using up and discarding each of its functional components. And one of the things plotting dehumanizes is the plotter himself. Become a tragic plotter and you are sure to be maligned. People will say you came into the world upside-down and gnashing like Richard Crookback, or they will long to bury you neck-deep in the earth like Aaron the Moor. If you become really good at plotting they will call you demi-devil, stare suspiciously at your feet, and stab you in a spirit of scientific inquiry.

Surely there is a paradox here. The aesthetic impulse is supposed to treat things not as means but as ends. It is supposed to paint fruit whose artfulness paralyzes the observer's salivary glands, to shape plays that convert the audience from Desdemona-rescuing Partridges into deeply moved but wisely passive Wordsworths. Very often, however, the aesthetic impulse does not work so gently in playwrights, who to achieve their aesthetic ends are notoriously ruthless in employing both people and characters. Playwriting tends to leave in its wake a lot of damp ex-friends muttering things like "If I had any idea he was going to put Andrew and me into his play as those dolts Aguecheek and Belch he'd have had damned fewer cakes and ale at our expense!" Nor is it any less ruthless with characters. Shakespeare's reworkings of Cinthio's tale—"Let me age and blacken the Moor, invent the gull Roderigo, erase Iago's genuine love for Desdemona, tone down the brutality of the murder, and get rid of the long horror story in which Desdemona's relatives take their revenge"— are as blandly manipulative as Iago's evil schemings: "Let me move Roderigo there, station Othello here, bring in Cassio with a handkerchief" and so on. Here again is motiveless malignity in the role of aesthetic disinterestedness—the kind of disinterestedness that exploits friend and foe alike, that humiliates and murders a Desdemona as readily as a Roderigo, and that steals from Cinthio, Plutarch, Holinshed, and Belleforest without a blush. When your aim is fine designs, everything is grist for the mill.

3. Satisfaction and Form

But fine designs do have drawbacks. The very reason perfect forms are aesthetically satisfying—because they are perfect—may also render them dissatisfying. They have achieved the state Othello claims for himself when he boasts of his "perfect soul" and the Senate calls him "all in all sufficient" (4.1.266). What is truly all in all sufficient—whether a person, a play, or a polyhedron—is closed off to the imagination and essentially dead. The closure of a curved line on itself gives birth to a circle but kills possibility; it leaves no openings, has no future, and while its closure may be deeply satisfying to the scientist, it cannot but make the critic grieve. Perhaps that is why Shakespeare associates Othello's moments of emotional repletion, his feeling of all in all sufficiency in war and love, with death.

If we adopt Kenneth Burke's psychological definition of form—"the creation of an appetite in the mind of the auditor, and the adequate satisfying of that appetite"[10]—then we can see in Shakespeare's craft a metadramatic parallel to Iago's craftiness. For Iago is busily engaged in creating an appetite in Othello. "Would I were satisfied!" Othello cries, and Iago, anxious to please, replies—

> I see, sir, you are eaten up with passion.
> I do repent me that I put it to you.
> You would be satisfied?
> OTH.   Would? Nay, and I will.
> IAGO   And may; but how? How satisfied, my lord?
> Would you, the supervisor, grossly gape on?
> Behold her topped?   (3.3.396)

As an interior playwright, Iago's business is to promise the satisfactions of a completed action but also to postpone their arrival. A small example occurs when Othello responds to the story about Cassio's sensual dream as though all his doubts were satisfied and only revenge remains: "I'll tear her all to pieces." But this is too easily accomplished; it offends Iago's artistic sensibilities. "Nay," he interrupts, "but be wise. Yet we see nothing done; / She may be honest yet." What an evil genius lies in those two *yets*, holding out as they do the tantalizing possibility that nothing has been done but factoring in a cynical assumption that even if it be not now, yet it will come; the readiness—a jealous anguish sustained at the level of almost-certainty, of almost-form—is all.

More widely, the action of the play begins on two fronts, love and war, with Othello apparently in command of both. However, the action of love seems less to begin than already to have concluded; we begin where comedies end, with man and maid already married. But *has* this action really been completed? At the risk of immodesty, we must ask how long were the newlyweds in the Sagittary, and what were they doing when Iago called Othello forth. In short, has the Moor actually bedded his wife?

Iago seems to answer these questions with his pruriencies about white ewes being tupped "even now, now, very now," but Iago knows no more than we do of the matter—he later queries Othello with the wink and nudge of one married man to another, "But, I pray you, sir, / Are you fast married?" (1.2.10). Iago doesn't know, the audience doesn't know, and as for Shakespeare, he keeps his counsel.

Thus it seems *theatrically* plausible that Desdemona remains unbedded or incompletely bedded throughout the play.[11] I say "theatrically" here in reference to the infamous "double time scheme," for as everyone knows the stage portrayal of events leaves no time for Cassio to bed Desdemona (if he is supposed to do so after the marriage), and as though to obviate this problem Shakespeare inserts various suggestions that a longer period of time has elapsed during which adultery could have been committed (and the marriage consummated).

Even without a double time scheme, however, the absence of an opportunity to commit adultery passes unnoticed in the theater simply because it is never mentioned ("Nonsense, how is this possible?") and because the audience knows it is a lie anyhow. On the other hand, the possibilities of an unconsummated marriage are clearly advertised: we hear of Othello's being called forth from the Sagittary on his wedding night; we hear his vehement denials of erotic desire before the Senate; we hear him assign Desdemona to a separate ship; we see their separation dramatized in the arrival of the ships at Cyprus; we hear him invite Desdemona to bed with the words "The purchase made, the fruits are to ensue; / The profit's yet to come 'tween me and you" (2.3.10); and we hear him accept with remarkable equanimity a second arousal from bed—" 'Tis the soldiers' life / To have their balmy slumbers waked with strife" (2.3.251).

In Burke's terms then, Shakespeare creates an appetite in the audience, a curiosity about the consummation of the marriage, that instead of being satisfied is sustained throughout the play. Not of course that we expect ocular proof—a theatrical reenactment of the moment when the gods gathered about to watch the net of Hephaestus drop on Ares and Aphrodite—but we might have expected something to negate the interruptions and separations that give us doubtful pause. As it is, we remain uncertain until the Murder Scene, when we obtain ocular proof indeed.[12] Grossly gaping on as Desdemona is at last bedded, we are perversely satisfied, for we find that satisfaction and death coincide—our satisfaction, Othello's satisfaction, Desdemona's death.

But is *satisfaction* really the right word? Do we actually take some kind of pleasure in the smothering of the innocent Desdemona? Alas, so it would seem. A pleasure analogous to that which I attributed to Shakespeare earlier: "How sad but how marvelously right!" As possibility evolves into probability and then into inevitability, a sense of formal completion yields aesthetic pleasure—the kind we experience when Oedipus is blinded, Faustus carried off, or Samson Agonistes crushed. Thus we too participate in that disinterestedness that borders on motiveless malignity. Not that heartless pleasure is all we feel. Rather, like Othello, we are torn between a soft-hearted pity for Desdemona and a stony-hearted devotion to a "cause" that requires her death to fulfill its destined logic.

Of course this stony-hearted aesthetic pleasure ought to be evoked at the end of any tragedy. But in *Othello* Shakespeare takes special pains to call it forth. It is a matter of satisfaction. In the previous chapter I mentioned that whether or not there is a *coitus interruptus* in the play there is certainly a *miles interruptus* when the anticipated battle with the Turks fails to materialize. Thus the energies that drive Othello toward his violent ends are generated, I argued, less by sexual than by martial frustrations.

Othello, however, is not the only person deprived of satisfaction by the disappearance of the Turks. We too have been led to expect a battle, to look forward to experiencing some measure of the pomp and glory and the downright violence that Othello speaks of later. But then, inexplicably, the Turks vanish in an offstage tempest, the battle comes to nought, and we must content ourselves with this weak piping time of peace.

Here is a perfect example of Burke's psychology of form subverted. An appetite is created in the audience, only to be frustrated. Precisely what we would expect of Iago, but the villain here is Shakespeare. What Iago keeps doing to Roderigo (and will later do to Othello), Shakespeare does to us. Curiously enough, precisely at this point Iago seeks to rekindle Roderigo's desire to put money in his purse by assuring him that Desdemona's marital content cannot last, that she already fancies Cassio:

> Mark me with what violence she first loved the Moor, but for bragging and telling her fantastical lies. And will she love him still for prating? Let not thy discreet heart think it. Her eye must be fed; and what delight shall she have to look on the devil? When the blood is made dull with the act of sport, there should be, again to inflame it and to give satiety a fresh appetite, loveliness in favor, sympathy

in years, manners, and beauties—all which the Moor is defective
in. (2.1.222–30)

Trust Iago to have made a study of desire and to know it arises from human defect. Humans are not complete, nor were meant to be; they lust because they want, and they want because they are wanting. That includes not merely the Desdemonas and Roderigos but us in the audience as well, who are here because we too lack and want, because we lack and therefore want form, eloquence, beauty, and, to be sure, the satisfactions and consummations of violence. But satisfaction is hard come by and harder kept. Satiety cannot succeed satiety without something to rekindle desire, and nothing kindles desire like frustration.

In some degree then, by playing on our desire for aesthetic form, for the completion of an action and the satisfaction of an appetite, Shakespeare seduces us into wanting Iago's violent plot to succeed. If we cannot have warfare between Turks and Venetians, let us have it elsewhere, in love and revenge. So the impulse to battle is displaced onto sex, issues of state divert into domestic channels, and violence to others turns reflexive. "Are we turned Turks," Othello demands of the rioters on Cyprus, "and to ourselves do that / Which heaven hath forbid the Ottomites?" (2.3.164). But this random drunken swordplay between Cassio and a few Cypriots is no substitute for the Turkish wars; only something with shape and tragic size to it can satisfy us now—and Othello too for that matter. "You would be satisfied?" Iago asks.

"Would? Nay, and I will."

And so he is. Increasingly it is he who is turned Turk on the painful wheel of Iago's lies, and this Turk will not disappear until he gets the violence he wants. Thus, killing a whore he has his revenge, and at the same time a perverted sexual climax. Iago too has his satisfaction as his plot rounds to a successful close. And as it succeeds, our formal desires are satisfied as well. The fatal bedding of Desdemona consummates the marriage and our aesthetic expectations at once. With Othello standing in for the Turk, and Desdemona for Cyprus, everyone rests content in the perfection of form. Except that . . .

4. Dissatisfaction and Unity

. . . as I said before, perfect form satisfies dissatisfyingly. Surely it does in *Othello*, where the perfection of Iago's and Shakespeare's plots entails the disintegration of perfection in the hero—the collapse of Othello's absolute content and all in all sufficiency. Yet even the perfection of those plots is called in doubt. The moment of success, when Othello is content that he has dealt harsh justice to a whore, and Iago is content that his design is complete, is shattered by Emilia's screechings of "Villainy!" Suddenly all is thrown into doubt and confusion, and as the satisfactions of completed action dissolve, it becomes apparent that no action is complete until it is understood, until the question "What has happened here?" is satisfactorily answered.

What *has* happened here?

Emilia discloses what she knows up to a point, the point of Iago's sword, which is still stained with the blood of Roderigo, who might have told far more. With both of them dead, only Iago knows the truth. "Will you, I pray, demand that demi-devil / Why he hath thus ensnared my soul and body?"

To which Iago famously replies, "From this time forth I never will speak word." And, true to his word for once, later on when Othello has increased the "tragic loading of this bed" with the weight of his own body and Lodovico declares "This is thy work" and pauses, or should pause, to invite an explanation, Iago says nothing.

What then are Lodovico and Gratiano to report to the Senate? The situation casts them jointly in the role of Horatio, commandeered by the dying Hamlet to tell his story to the yet unknowing world. Horatio's is no easy task, even though Hamlet had earlier filled in the gaps of the story for his friend by passing on the Ghost's tale, for instance, and by recounting the ocean voyage episode. But Lodovico and Gratiano have a more difficult task, for the biggest gaps in their knowledge of Othello's story—the events that occurred back in Venice and the temptation of Othello by Iago—although they could be, will not be filled in by the schemer who was there. When Iago lapses into silence Othello's story disappears too—or would have if it weren't for some incriminating messages conveniently discovered in the pockets of Roderigo and Iago: a couple of letters passed between the two villains plus "a discontented paper" of Iago's. These provide just enough information to call forth from Othello a breast-beating "O fool, fool, fool!"

But letters must be interpreted, because as recent philosophy has made abundantly clear, writing keeps its intentions to itself. Refusing to answer questions, to explain itself, it says only "What

you know, you know," or "What is written is written," and with-
draws into an Iago-like silence. Shakespeare's play is similarly unre-
sponsive, and for a similar reason. For despite its dialogue and
speeches, it is as much a written document as that original focus of
hermeneutics, the Bible. The actor who plays Iago can no more
answer our questions than the villain he plays. His speech is not
authentic speech, an invitation to dialogue, but spoken writing; and
we know Hamlet's opinion of those who "speak more than is set
down for them"—"That's villainous!"

If Hamlet the dramaturge is right, then Iago is no villain. He
says precisely what is set down for him, no more, no less. And what is
set down for him is nothing—which accords perfectly with the fact
that no one knows better than he that there *is* nothing, no definitive
truth, to repeat at this point, even if he wanted to repeat it. As the
very spirit of mediation he knows that the act of reaching out for
knowledge fends it off, that ocular proof is blind and certainty uncertain. Iago stands for nothing—or, rather, for Nothing, for the negative that shadows all positives. Thus his first gesture of deception
takes the form of "Ha! I like not that" as Cassio departs (3.3.35).
Then to Othello's "What dost thou say?" he replies "Nothing, my
lord; or, if—I know not what." In these first two lines of his as
tempter, he issues three negatives—two *nots* and one *nothing*—and
one curious positive negative, *know*. These supply us with our first
hint of the *no* lurking within *know*, of the fact that Iago's insinuations,
in a diabolic version of creation ex nihilo, mold the empty substance
of "nothing" into the illusion of its homonym "noting."

Othello picks up this negative style immediately by saying,
not as we would expect "Was that Cassio?" but "Was *not* that Cassio
parted from my wife?" The repetition of *not* is insidious for two reasons—because it casts the shadow of *naught* across both Othello's discourse and Desdemona's conduct, precisely the shadow Iago wants to
have cast, and because its presence here precludes a true answer to
Othello's question. Had Othello said "Was that Cassio?" a straightforward "Yes" would have delivered the truth. Phrased as it is,
however, a reply of "Yes" would merge bafflingly with "No," since it
could mean either "Yes, it was not" or "Yes, it was." But Iago always
avoids the word *yes*, even when it would prove cunningly ambiguous.
In this case he replies typically with another question—"Cassio, my
lord?"—and then drifts into troubled conjecture: "No, sure, I cannot think it."

Inasmuch as Othello's "Was not that Cassio parted from my wife?" invites an equivocal response it forecasts his later ambivalence. He wants ocular proof and an end to doubt, yet he covets ignorance and blindness. He would have been happy, he says, if the "entire camp" had "tasted her sweet body, / So I had nothing known" (3.3.351). No in-betweens for him—he would know either everything or nothing; and his desire here to know nothing leads inevitably to his obliteration of all offensive knowledge in an epileptic loss of consciousness. The irony of course lies in the fact that, as with all of Iago's lies, there is nothing to be known. "By heaven, I'll know thy thoughts!" Othello demands, but Iago's dark thoughts cannot be brought to light, because, quite simply, he has no dark thoughts about Desdemona.

At the same time Iago specializes in the knowledge of the unacknowledged. He knows and suggests with sidelong smiles and dark hints what, he implies, all Venetians know but never express, that all men are knaves and lechers at heart, all women whores, and under the lapel of every virtue is a sales tag. Such knowing is negative by necessity—unacknowledged knowledge, the truths culture says "no" to in order to survive as culture.

But Iago knows, and plays the knowing game to perfection. "Good sir, be a man," he implores Othello:

> Think every bearded fellow that's but yoked
> May draw with you. There's millions now alive
> That nightly lie in those unproper beds
> Which they dare swear peculiar; your case is better.
> O, 'tis the spite of hell, the fiend's arch-mock,
> To lip a wanton in a secure couch,
> And to suppose her chaste. *No*, let me *know;*
> And *knowing* what I am, I *know* what she shall be.   (4.1.65)

Every *know* that comes into Iago's gravitational field here is warped into a *no*, so that "knowing what I am" becomes a kind of *no-ing* or nullifying of self in the sacred act of achieving self-knowledge. What can be known, contra Othello, is not what one is but only what one is not, as Iago declared earlier when he said "I am not what I am." Then, with this non-knowledge of self intact, he will "know what she shall be." Here the *no* within *know* not merely nullifies self-knowledge but destroys the self—"what she shall be" is no-thing, a whore, a dead whore.

The nullity at the center of knowing is brought forth climactically when Iago's knowledge of Othello's story is demanded, and he delivers his tautological reply,

> Demand me nothing. What you know, you know.
> From this time forth I never will speak word.

Absorbing some of the negative radiation from *nothing* in the first sentence and *never* in the third, the otherwise invisible *no* within the twice repeated *know* of the second sentence begins to glow with an oxymoronic, cross-canceling energy. To *know* is to *no*, to deny; knowledge in this bad world is self-negating—what you know cannot be acknowledged. Since society is grounded on that which is unspoken, I shall not speak. Or, inversely, what you *no* you *know*—what you negate by a failure to acknowledge, you nevertheless *do* know, we all do; hence explanations are superfluous. Make of it what you will.

So the truth we are so anxious to know (whatever words like that might mean after Iago's final speech) dissolves into silence. Not, however, Emilia. Under the force of her clamoring accusations, Iago's seemingly perfect plot shatters. Of course this destruction of Iago's plot contributes to the construction of Shakespeare's. Not even Shakespeare's plot is perfect, however. In fact, if Iago's last speech undermines the concept of a causal beginning, Othello's last speech undermines the concept of an actional end; and both combine to make an assault on formal perfection.

As I said before, no action is complete until it is understood. Unfortunately no action is ever completely understood, for the signs of its understanding, the terms of its definition, are unending; there is always more that could be said. Every action, however unequivocal in appearance, attenuates into a series of fragmentary and conflicting interpretations or, less contentiously, flows into a sea of discourse.

That Shakespeare is conscious of this seems evident from Othello's closing address, which constitutes the first interpretation of his unlucky deeds. The first, for his is by no means the final story—in fact not even a story at all, but hints and instructions to those who will tell his story: "Then must you speak of. . . ." But hints and instructions must be interpreted, just as the letters Lodovico and Gratiano are shortly to write must be interpreted by the senators who read them. Othello's "unlucky deeds" forge a link in a chain of interpretation that stretches as far as this book and, however astonishing and painful to contemplate, even beyond.

5. Theatrical Property

We could put these matters in terms of property—theatrical property. In Chapter 2 I mentioned that theft could be regarded as a kind of communicative process in reverse, in which the sequence "sender-message-receiver" becomes "owner-property-thief." Translating *message* into *property* merely brings out a metaphor already latent in the sender-message-receiver formulation. For that sequence suggests that verbal expressions are, as messages, somewhat objectlike or propertylike; they bottle up meanings and pass them inviolate from person to person irrespective of speaker, hearer, or context.[13] Like an Aristotelean plot, there is a distinct beginning, middle, and end to such a process, and an element of shared ownership: my private ideas, packaged and shipped to you, become yours as well.

This notion of meaning as either private or public property seems written into *Othello*. That is, questions about ownership of property in the play, such as "Who owns Roderigo's purse or Othello's handkerchief?" or most critically "Who owns Desdemona herself?" give rise to the larger question, "Who owns *Othello?*"

The answer depends on who does the answering. Othello, advocate of unitary truths and private property, would reply "Shakespeare, of course." But a jurist of the day would have been less certain. He might have pointed out that a script in itself, however valuable, was not really property, although the writer had personal rights to it. But of course Shakespeare did not keep his script to himself; he sold it to his acting company for from six to ten pounds. Only then, "in the hands of an acting company," Joseph Loewenstein notes, "did the work begin to acquire abstract property values that needed protection: the right to exclusive performance and the right to control the reproduction of the manuscript, either by release to a scrivener or by sale of a copy to a printer or publisher."[14] Normally once the script had been sold to an acting company the playwright no longer had any rights in it. But the ownership of *Othello* would have been complicated by the fact that Shakespeare was, like Iago, something of a Johannes factotum of the theater—not only playwright and actor but also shareholder in his company and householder of the Globe. Thus he was selling his script in part to himself and buying it in part from himself. To the (let us say) ten pounds he got for *Othello* (a ten-pound play if ever there was one!) he could pocket his share of the take as actor (if he played a role) and as shareholder-householder as well, not to mention his share of the modest fee (two or three pounds) paid by a stationer to print it, had any printer done so during his lifetime. Thus, although he would still have a manifold financial interest in *Othello*, his authorial property rights, as we understand them today, were not so much forfeited as simply nonexistent to begin with.

And quite properly so, Iago would have said, thinking along other lines. For if Othello would answer "Shakespeare, of course" to the question "Who owns *Othello?*," Iago would surely demur—

> Shakespeare, my lord? No, sure, I cannot think it. Let me remind you that this fellow Shakespeare is himself little better than a thief. How do you think this script came into his keeping? I'll tell you. This piratical Stratfordian boarded a land-carrack named the *Hecatommithi*, captained by one Giovanni Battista Giraldi Cinthio, an honest countryman of mine, and, without so much as a "By your leave," he plucked a precious story from its hold, pocketed it up, and went his way. Oh, I grant you, he may have improved on it somewhat, but that does not make it his, any more than your marrying Desdemona made her yours. After all, she passed from her father to you and, so it seemed, from you to Cassio and (who knows?) perhaps to the entire camp, pioners and all. These stories, my lord, are like these women; we can call the creatures ours, but not their appetites. Look to't.

Translated from the Italian, Iago apparently means that Shakespeare can add to, subtract from, divide, and multiply Cinthio's story in an effort to make it his own—he can funnel into it his own meanings to suit his own designs and declare "This play is *my* play, as true a reflection of my truth as Desdemona is of Othello's, as unchanging as she, and . . ."—and, alas, as doomed to death as she. To claim the play as his private property, the repository of his fixed and constant truths, is to deprive it of its theatrical life and transform a live script into a dead text. The mode of existence of a play, insofar as it is based on sharing, discourages even the thought of authorial property rights. Even to bring it to theatrical being, the playwright must yield it up, first to the players and then to the audience, all of whom will swarm aboard and make off with chests of meanings they will claim for their own. The players are to the playwright who hands them his script as the listening Lodovico and Gratiano are to the Othello who tells them his version of his story. And lined up behind the players is a series of audiences who, like the senators back in Venice, will hear of these matters and interpret them each in its own way. This being the case, Shakespeare can no more claim exclusive title to his play than Othello can to his identity.

This does not mean that Shakespeare renounces his ownership entirely, although his apparent indifference to the publication of his plays might suggest as much. His modesty, I imagine, is on the sly side, as if he were to admit that his play is no more than a strumpet, as Pandarus implies at the end of *Troilus and Cressida* when he bequeaths the audience his diseases. But in *Othello* the strumpet Bianca longs for marriage to Cassio, and the so-called strumpet Desdemona is in reality true to her troth. Like the Desdemona of Othello's imagination, the play may "turn, and turn, and yet go on / And turn again," proving almost wantonly obedient to all who pay the fee and enjoy its favors. But of course these turnings are not as degrading as they might sound. The inconstancy of the play is a measure of its vitality. From age to age it is revivified in the interpretive imaginations of audiences. If it loses the integrity of a fixed monument in this process, it gains the integrity of an ever-changing but constant fountain.

Moreover, like a fountain its randomness is in some degree constrained by its source. Or, to return to the marriage metaphor, the play is also faithfully plighted to Shakespeare. It keeps its troth in the sense that it, like Sonnet 76, remains "so far from variation or quick change . . . That every word doth almost tell [his] name." No one but he could have made it so, and no matter how hospitable it is to our interpretive incursions, we cannot have it entirely as we like it. Like language itself, the play may be something of a strumpet, but in the keeping of a husband like Shakespeare it is also something of a beloved and honest wife. If it is no one's exclusive property, neither is it everyone's common goods.

Notes

I. Introduction

1   Kenneth Burke, "*Othello:* An Essay to Illustrate a Method," *Hudson Review* 4 (1951): 165–203. See also Mark Rose's brief but illuminating discussion of property and possession in "Othello's Occupation: Shakespeare and the Romance of Chivalry," *English Literary Renaissance* 15, no. 3 (Autumn 1985): 302–6; Juliet Dusinberre's informative chapter on women as property in Shakespeare's England—in her *Shakespeare and the Nature of Women* (London and Basingstroke: Macmillan, 1975); and Peter Stallybrass's brilliant study of "Patriarchal Territories: The Body Enclosed," which also takes Kenneth Burke as a starting point for a discussion of *Othello*—in *Rewriting the Renaissance*, ed. Margaret W. Ferguson, Maureen Quilligan, and Nancy J. Vickers (Chicago and London: University of Chicago Press, 1986), pp. 123–42. Finally, I have profited from some shrewd observations about property by James P. Carse in his *Finite and Infinite Games* (New York: The Free Press, 1986), pp. 41–47.

2   S. B. Liljegren, *The Fall of the Monasteries and the Social Changes in England Leading up to the Great Revolution*, pp. 130–31; cited by L. C. Knights, *Drama and Society in the Age of Jonson* (1937; New York: W. W. Norton, 1968), p. 101.

3   Robert L. Heilbroner, *The Worldly Philosophers*, 4th ed. (New York: Simon and Schuster, 1972), pp. 25–26.

4   See Mary Douglas, *Purity and Danger: An Analysis of the Concepts of Pollution and Taboo* (London: Routledge and Kegan Paul, 1966), esp. pp. 1–6.

5   For an excellent account of England's social, political, and legal attitudes toward outsiders, see Richard Marienstras's chapter "The Status of Foreigners under James I" in his *New Perspectives on the Shakespeare World*, trans. Janet Lloyd (Cambridge: Cambridge University Press, 1985), pp. 99–125. See also G. K. Hunter, "Elizabethans and Foreigners," *Shakespeare Survey* 17 (1964): 37–52.

6   Marienstras, *New Perspectives*, p. 114.

136 Notes to Introduction

7   Tzvetan Todorov, *The Conquest of America: The Question of the Other*, trans. Richard Howard (New York: Harper and Row, 1984). This barbaric treatment of barbarians was not of course universally condoned, as Montaigne's *Essays*, especially that on cannibals, testifies. Moreover, a certain noble savagism was also present, as G. K. Hunter records in "Othello and Colour Prejudice," *Proceedings of the British Academy* 53 (1967): 155–57.

8   Keith Thomas, *Man and the Natural World* (New York: Pantheon Books, 1983), pp. 36–37.

9   For the Protestant associations of the Devil with dirt, especially scatological dirt, see Luther's *Table-Talk* in H. Grisar, *Luther*, trans. E. M. Lamond, ed. L. Cappadelta, 6 vols. (London: Kegan Paul, Trench, Trubner, 1913–1917), vol. 6. See also "The Protestant Era" in Norman O. Brown, *Life Against Death* (New York: Vintage Books, 1959), pp. 202–33. In this connection, however, G. K. Hunter argues that Shakespeare systematically undermined the traditional association of black with evil—see "Othello and Colour Prejudice."

10   M. R. Ridley, introduction to *Othello*, Arden edition (Welwyn Garden City, Hertfordshire: Broadwater Press, 1958), pp. l–liii.

11   Marienstras, *New Perspectives*, p. 136.

12   P. L. Hughes and J. F. Larkin, *Tudor Royal Proclamations* (New Haven and London: Yale University Press, 1964–1969), 3:221; cited by Marienstras, ibid., p. 136. For studies of racist feelings in Shakespeare's England, see Eldred Jones, *Othello's Countrymen* (London: Oxford University Press, 1965) and *The Elizabethan Image of Africa* (Charlottesville: University of Virginia Press, 1971), and Winthrop Jordan, *The White Man's Burden: Historical Origins of Racism in the United States* (New York: Oxford University Press, 1974). With special reference to *Othello*, see G. K. Hunter, "Othello and Colour Prejudice," pp. 139–63; Doris Adler, "The Rhetoric of *Black* and *White* in *Othello*," *Shakespeare Quarterly* 25 (1974): 248–57; Harold Clarke Goddard, "*Othello* and the Race Problem," in his *Alphabet of the Imagination* (Atlantic Highlands, N.J.: Humanities Press, 1974), pp. 74–84; Martin Orkin, "*Othello* and the 'plain face' of Racism," *Shakespeare Quarterly* 38 (Summer 1987): 166–88; and Karen Newman, " 'And Wash the Ethiop White': Femininity and the Monstrous in *Othello*," in *Shakespeare Reproduced*, ed. Jean E. Howard and Marion F. O'Connor (New York and London: Methuen, 1987), pp. 143–62.

13   Hunter, "Othello and Colour Prejudice," 147.

14   Norman Rabkin gives full critical scope to Othello's Christianity in *Shakespeare and the Common Understanding* (New York: The Free Press, 1967), pp. 57–73—e.g., "Nowhere else in Shakespeare are we led to think more explicitly in Christian terms. Of all the tragic heroes Othello is the most emphatically Christian. . . . What really matters is not the fact that Othello is a devoted Christian, but the fact that his love for Desdemona is a version of the Christian faith" (p. 63).

15 The various meanings of *proper* can be found both in the *OED* and in C. T. Onions, *A Shakespeare Glossary*, 2d ed. (Oxford: Clarendon Press, 1919). Those who construe *proper* to mean handsome probably do so on the example of Emilia's replying "A very handsome man" when Desdemona later observes that "This Lodovico is a proper man" (4.3.38).

16 Nietzsche: "It is obvious that everywhere the designations of moral value were at first applied to *men*, and were only derivatively and at a later period applied to *actions*" (*Beyond Good and Evil*, chap. 9, sec. 260).

17 See Ernst Cassirer, *Mythical Thought*, trans. Ralph Manheim, vol. 2 of *The Philosophy of Symbolic Forms* (New Haven: Yale University Press, 1955). In *The Ethic of Time* (New York: Seabury Press, 1976), pp. 118 ff., Wylie Sypher suggests that Othello experiences a fall from a magical, mythical identity with the world to a state of tragic isolation because when Iago teaches him to think, "he finds that he is alien—black, different, abused" (p. 119).

18 Lawrence Stone *The Crisis of the Aristocracy, 1558–1641* (Oxford: Oxford University Press, 1965), p. 613.

19 The "profits" metaphor runs throughout *The Merchant of Venice* in the form of "use." In the sonnets *profit* becomes *increase*, which from fairest creatures we desire (Sonnet 1), else "beauty's treasure" goes for nought (Sonnet 6).

20 "It is more than a little tempting," Mark Rose says, "to think of Iago as an embodiment of the prodigious energies of the new commercialism of the Renaissance, and thus to turn *Othello* into an allegory in which bourgeois man destroys the representative of the older feudal values" ("Othello's Occupation," p. 300).

21 Stone, *Crisis of the Aristocracy*, p. 158.

22 Oddly enough, money was becoming common in England at the same time that the pistol and rapier were—weapons that Lawrence Stone says served as social equalizers in this violent period (ibid., p. 245). The disruptiveness of money to the social hierarchy is most evident in the prevalence of usury. Malynes's tract on usury (*Saint George for England* [1601]) opens with a description of how the Dragon of usury "overthroweth the harmony of the strings of the good government of a commonwealth, by too much enriching some, and by oppressing and impoverishing some others, bringing the instrument out of tune: when as every member of the same should live contented in his vocation and execute his charge according to his profession." Cited by Knights in *Drama and Society in the Age of Jonson*, p. 146.

23 See W. H. Auden, *The Dyer's Hand and Other Essays* (New York: Random House, 1962), p. 220.

24 For an exhaustive treatment of bestial imagery—and for that matter of any other imagery—in the play, see Robert B. Heilman's *Magic in the Web* (Lexington: University of Kentucky Press, 1956). Since my debt to

Heilman's classic study of the play is so pervasive that I'm sure to have failed to record numerous local instances of it, let me issue a blanket IOU at this point.

II. Property, Violence, and Women

1   Bertram O'States, *Othello*, Dun Aengus Shakespeare Series (Corca Dhuibhne: Contiga Press, 1987), p. 1234. I might add that the tone of this editorial note helps explain why Professor O'States has often been called the Thersites of Shakespearean scholarship.

2   Perhaps I should explain the prevalence of plural pronouns here and elsewhere in this book. Torn between the Scylla of a royal *we* and the Charybdis of a self-advertising *I*, I have often opted for an alternative *we*, one that jettisons royal authority ("What cares these roarers for the name of king?") and pretends to speak for those of us who are simply in the same boat together struggling to figure out what is going on, or down. "Pretends" because such a *we* gives the illusion of an audience whose response to the play is (as the singularity of "audience" and "response" implies) unified, despite diversities of age, race, gender, and personal disposition. Such an audience is, needless to say, a fiction. My use of *we*, then, is simply an invitation to the reader to share a particular perspective on *Othello*, after which she is perfectly free to go her own way. Which is to say, as Molloy said of the impermeability of the *Times Literary Supplement*, "Damn it, I should never have mentioned it."

3   René Girard, *Deceit, Desire, and the Novel*, trans. Yvonne Freccero (Baltimore and London: Johns Hopkins University Press, 1965).

4   See Michael Neill's illuminating analysis, "Changing Places in *Othello*," *Shakespeare Survey* 37 (1978): 122.

5   G. K. Hunter remarks that "there is a powerful line of criticism on *Othello*, going back at least as far as A. W. Schlegel [*Lectures on Dramatic Art* (1815), 2:189], that paints the Moor as savage at heart, one whose veneer of Christianity and civilization cracks as the play proceeds, to reveal and liberate his basic savagery" ("Othello and Colour Prejudice," p. 159). Or as Dieter Mehl puts it, "The confrontation between Othello and Iago powerfully suggests the idea of barbarian animal forces, temporarily brought under control by the Moor's integration into the Christian community, but ready to erupt again at any time, like the Turks" (*Shakespeare's Tragedies: An Introduction* [Cambridge: Cambridge University Press, 1983], p. 68). But of course the point is that this barbarity, if it lies dormant in the Moor, is already virulently active in that respected citizen of civilized Venice, Iago. As I say, barbarity cannot be confined to Othello's personality; it is in the play at large, overtly in Iago, covertly elsewhere—for instance, within the civilized concepts of property and marriage.

6   Erich Fromm, *The Heart of Man* (New York: Harper and Row, 1964), p. 117.

7   James Hall, *Dictionary of Subjects and Symbols in Art* (New York: Harper and Row, 1974), p. 61. "This creature, half-man and half-horse, has always symbolized lust," according to Beryl Rowland in *Animals with Human Faces: A Guide to Animal Symbolism* (Knoxville: University of Tennessee Press, 1973), p. 53. Recalling Lear's famous lines about woman being centaurish "down from the waist" (4.6.124), we might assume that the Sagittary could be associated with Desdemona rather than or as well as with Othello. But all the equine imagery in *Othello* comes to focus on the Moor, not his wife; and, moreover, as Rowland observes of the centaur figure, "He was an archer, and traditionally, as may be seen in the Pentateuch, the bow and arrow *(keschess)*, was often used as the symbol for the normal male act of *ejaculatio seminis.*"

8   On a somewhat similar occasion, the centaur Nessus persuaded Hercules to swim across a river while he himself promised to ferry his wife Deianeira across. Once Hercules reached the far bank, however, Nessus attempted to ravish Deianeira, but was slain by one of Hercules's arrows. See Ovid's version, *Metamorphoses*, 9: 101–33.

9   Hall, *Dictionary of Subjects and Symbols in Art*, p. 61.

10   As David Bevington observes, "In [Act 1, Scene 2] Othello too appears with Iago and *'Attendants with torches,'* in a scene that is visually parallel [to Act 1, Scene 1]; yet the tiring-house now represents the inn called the Sagittary where Othello stays with Desdemona. . . . The striking visual repetition underscores the seriousness of Desdemona's choice as she moves from her father's world to that of Othello" (*Action Is Eloquence: Shakespeare's Language of Gesture* [Cambridge, Mass., and London, England: Harvard University Press, 1984], p. 111).

11   Jean Genet, *The Thief's Journal*, trans. Bernard Frechtman (New York: Grove Press, 1964), p. 139.

12   In Genet's case the intoxication is also of course sexual—theft is a form of rape, a "having" in both senses; but sex for Genet seems always to be associated with a deeper desire to unite with the other by stealing his being.

13   Michael Neill observantly notes the pun on *ewe/you* here, in "Changing Places in *Othello*," p. 122.

14   The parallel with Shylock is additionally interesting in that when Jessica steals her father's ducats and especially his two "stones"— literally the family jewels (2.8.20)—she steals, what the loss of Desdemona seems also to imply, his virility and very nearly his life. Another interesting connection between the two plays is the stereotypical denomination of the Jew as "black." As Sander L. Gilman remarks, "the association of the Jew with blackness is as old as Christian tradition. Medieval iconography always

juxtaposed the black image of the 'synagogue,' of the 'Old Law,' with the white of the Church" (*Difference and Pathology* [Ithaca and London: Cornell University Press, 1985], p. 31).

15   See Elias Canetti's section, "The Survivor," in his *Crowds and Power*, trans. Carol Stewart (1962; New York: Continuum, 1973), pp. 227–77.

16   See in this respect Ruth Levitsky, "All-In-All Sufficiency in *Othello*," *Shakespeare Studies* 6 (1970): 209–21. She associates Othello's all-in-allness with Stoic independence, which is presumably nearer to Aristotle's godlikeness than to the bestiality of self-sufficient Machiavellian evil. Aristotle's remark appears in the *Politics* (Book 1, 2).

17   Dusinberre, *Shakespeare and the Nature of Women*, pp. 111, 113–16. Pleasure stood outside the margin of the Puritan work ethic just as woman stood outside the pure inner circle of masculinity.

18   Coppélia Kahn centers her discussion of *Othello* in this fearful expectation of cuckoldry on the part of husbands; see *Man's Estate: Masculine Identity in Shakespeare* (Berkeley and Los Angeles: University of California Press, 1981), pp. 140–46.

19   In fact Carol Thomas Neely makes the rather astonishing claim that Emilia "is dramatically and symbolically the play's fulcrum," because "the play's central theme is love—specifically marital love—[and] its central conflict is between the men and the women . . ." (*Broken Nuptials in Shakespeare's Plays* [New Haven and London: Yale University Press, 1985], p. 108). Iago himself would probably protest that far from being central to the action his wife is merely a weapon he employs in his own war against Othello. But Professor Neely might reply that such a claim illustrates the very misogyny she finds central to the play. Unfortunately, a predisposition to define central themes and conflicts runs the risk of setting up structuralist oppositions of an either/or variety that elide nuances of character and conduct, especially in a play that seems bent on deconstructing unities. Thus Neely finds the men in the play uniformly "murderous . . . foolishly idealistic or anxiously cynical" (p. 114), dominated by "vanity, rivalry, and dependence" (p. 118), and characterized by "cowardice, clumsiness, and insecurity" (p. 121), whereas the very rare feminine shortcoming is either attributed to masculine domination (sometimes quite properly so) or overlooked. For instance, Emilia's callous willingness to stand by while Desdemona is tormented by Othello about the lost handkerchief (3.4.51–100) goes unremarked, even though her behavior at that point rivals Iago's cruelty in the postbrothel scene (4.2.111–73).

20   Ian Maclean, *The Renaissance Notion of Woman* (Cambridge: Cambridge University Press, 1980), p. 8.

21   This lightning-rod effect is attributed by William Empson to comic subplots in Renaissance drama—see *Some Versions of Pastoral* (New

York: New Directions, 1960), pp. 25–84—and by Robert Penn Warren to "impure poetry" in "Pure and Impure Poetry," *Kenyon Review,* 5 (Spring 1943): 228–54. Kenneth Burke follows this line too in his remarks about Emilia in "Othello: An Essay to Illustrate a Method," pp. 172–74.

22   Shirley Nelson Garner, "Shakespeare's Desdemona," *Shakespeare Studies* 9 (1976): 247.

23   On the other hand, see Ian Maclean, who, in his "Conclusion" to *The Renaissance Notion of Woman,* cites the forces that militated for and against the improvement of women's status (pp. 82–92) but who, incidentally, does not mention the liberating influence of Puritanism emphasized by Juliet Dusinberre, *Shakespeare and the Nature of Women,* esp. pp. 77–136.

24   Robert G. Hunter, *Shakespeare and the Mystery of God's Judgments* (Athens: University of Georgia Press, 1976), p. 151.

25   In matters of gender, as in all others, it seems, Shakespeare is various and elusive, neither a mouthpiece for conservative beliefs nor a rebel against them, inclined to shift his focus depending on the genre he works in (as Linda Bamber argues in *Comic Women, Tragic Men: A Study of Gender and Genre in Shakespeare* [Palo Alto: Stanford University Press, 1982]). For Marilyn French, however, Shakespeare is a relatively unresisting conduit for the male chauvinism of his day—*Shakespeare's Division of Experience* (New York: Summit Books, 1981); and for Madelon Gohlke, even when Shakespeare seems sympathetic to feminine issues, he is merely providing a "rationale for the structure of male dominance"—see "'I wooed thee with my sword': Shakespeare's Tragic Paradigms," in *Representing Shakespeare: New Psychoanalytic Essays,* ed. Murray Schwartz and Coppélia Kahn (Baltimore: Johns Hopkins University Press, 1980), p. 180. On the other hand Juliet Dusinberre argues that "Shakespeare saw men and women as equal in a world which declared them unequal. He did not divide human nature into the masculine and the feminine, but observed in the individual woman or man an infinite variety of union between opposing impulses" (*Shakespeare and the Nature of Women,* p. 308). Those who, in varying degrees, regard Shakespeare as a writer resistant to the conventional gender expectations of his time would also include Marianne Novy, *Love's Argument: Gender Relations in Shakespeare* (Chapel Hill and London: University of North Carolina Press, 1984); Kahn, *Man's Estate;* Lisa Jardine, *Still Harping on Daughters: Women and Drama in the Age of Shakespeare* (Brighton and Totowa, N.J.: Harvester Press and Barnes & Noble, 1983); and Jonathan Goldberg, "Shakespearean Inscriptions: The Voicing of Power," in *Shakespeare and the Question of Theory,* ed. Patricia Parker and Geoffrey Hartman (New York and London: Methuen, 1985), pp. 116–37. With regard to Desdemona, Karen Newman says that although she suffers the "conventional fate assigned to the desiring woman . . . Shakespeare's representation of her as at once virtuous and desiring, and of her choice in love as heroic rather than demonic, dislocates the conventional

ideology of gender the play also enacts" ("'And wash the Ethiop white':
Femininity and the Monstrous in *Othello*," p. 158).

26   In "The Design of Desdemona: Doubt Raised and Resolved,"
Shakespeare Studies 13 (1980): 187–96, Ann Jennalie Cook examines doubts
the audience may have about the propriety of Desdemona's conduct at this
early point (Is she a sexual outlaw indulging her own desires or an idealized
image of feminine love?)—doubts that place the audience in a position
analogous to that of Othello when Iago renders his wife's identity ambiguous.

27   Or, as Carol Thomas Neely says, "Desdemona's spirit, clarity,
and realism do not desert her entirely in the latter half of the play as many
critics and performances imply"—"Women and Men in *Othello*," *Shakespeare Studies* 10 (1977): 141.

28   The remark by Simone Weill is cited by Erich Fromm in *The
Heart of Man*, p. 40.

29   I follow QI's "utmost pleasure" here instead of F's "very quality," for the reasons outlined by Ridley in the Arden text (p. 35)—and of
course because "utmost pleasure" echoes in our minds appropriately at this
uttermost point in Desdemona's experience.

III. Appalling Property

1   Shakespeare was hardly alone in finding love's fusions of disparate identities puzzling, as Donne's lines in "The Canonization" attest:
   The Phoenix riddle hath more wit
   By us, we two being one, are it.
So, to one neutrall thing both sexes fit.
For a few brief but typically brilliant remarks about how property is appalled
in "The Phoenix and the Turtle," see Murray Krieger, *A Window to Criticism: Shakespeare's Sonnets and Modern Poetics* (Princeton: Princeton University Press, 1964), pp. 150–54.

2   Particularly impressive discussions of how love in the sonnets
and comedies bears on *Othello* are those by Rosalie Colie, *Shakespeare's Living
Art* (Princeton: Princeton University Press, 1974), pp. 135–67; by Susan
Snyder, *The Comic Matrix of Shakespeare's Tragedies* (Princeton: Princeton
University Press, 1979), pp. 70–90, especially with respect to exchanges of
identity; and by Richard P. Wheeler, "' . . . And my loud crying still': The
Sonnets, The Merchant of Venice, and *Othello*," in *Shakespeare's "Rough
Magic": Renaissance Essays in Honor of C. L. Barber*, ed. Peter Erickson and
Coppélia Kahn (Newark: University of Delaware Press, 1985), pp. 193–209,
esp. pp. 201 ff.

3   Lawrence Stone, *Crisis of the Aristocracy*, pp. 589–669. As Ann
Jennalie Cook remarks, "Marriage without parental consent was specifically
forbidden to anyone under the age of twenty-one according to the canon law

of 1603" ("The Design of Desdemona," p. 188). Carol Thomas Neely makes the point that the fixed marriage by no means disappeared with the arrival of the companionate marriage (*Broken Nuptials in Shakespeare's Plays*, pp. 9–11).

4 Little wonder Elizabethan husbands spent so much time inspecting their foreheads: the fixed marriage practically guaranteed their monstering. In Shakespeare, however, despite all the talk about cuckoldry, the horned thing itself rarely appears. The fixed marriage seems an instance of a cultural practice fostering behavior that is then labeled natural and made a reason for perpetuating the practice. That is, such mismatches encouraged adultery in women (in men it was ignored), thereby attesting to their carnal nature and proving the need for further marriages made by economically watchful parents rather than by the young people themselves for "companionship" (i.e., sexual desire). The double standard was often inveighed against in Emilia's style but remained securely intact—see Keith Thomas, "The Double Standard," *Journal of the History of Ideas* 20 (1959): 195–216.

5 Leo Kirschbaum, "The Modern Othello," *English Literary History* 2 (1944): 291; reprinted in *A Casebook on Othello*, ed. Leonard F. Dean (New York: Thomas Y. Crowell, 1961), p. 163. Richard P. Wheeler puts it more accurately: "When Othello marries Desdemona, he makes of her a compassionate mirror of his own heroic status ('She loved me for the dangers I had passed, / And I loved her that she did pity them' [1.3.167–68]"—in his "' . . . And my loud crying still,'" p. 203 (see also p. 204 for an insightful discussion of Othello's mirrorings).

6 Graham Bradshaw, *Shakespeare's Skepticism* (New York: St. Martin's Press, 1987), p. 4.

7 G. W. F. Hegel, *Phenomenology of Spirit*, trans. A. V. Miller (Oxford: Clarendon Press, 1977), p. 111; cited by Malcolm Evans in *Signifying Nothing* (Athens: University of Georgia Press, 1986), p. 76.

8 See Freud, *A General Introduction to Psycho-Analysis*, trans. J. Riviere (New York: Perma Giants, 1953), pp. 60–62, and *New Introductory Lectures on Psycho-Analysis*, trans. W. J. H. Sprott (London: Hogarth Press and The Institute of Psycho-Analysis, 1933), p. 86.

9 Regarding the "mirror stage": Jacques Lacan, *Ecrits: A Selection* (New York: Norton, 1977), pp. 1–7.

10 Stephen J. Greenblatt, *Renaissance Self-Fashioning: From More to Shakespeare* (Chicago and London: University of Chicago Press, 1980). It may not be accidental that the concept of the unified self came into being during a period in which the quality of mirrors improved greatly, as Yi-Fu Tuan suggests in *Segmented Worlds and Self* (Minneapolis: University of Minnesota Press, 1982), p. 163.

11 "Beneath his apparent self-confidence," writes Carol McGinnis Kay, "is a void of genuine confidence. In fact, Othello exhibits what psychol-

ogists call an 'immature ego.'" See "Othello's Need for Mirrors," *Shakespeare Quarterly* 34, no. 3 (Autumn 1983): 263. This of course is the burden of Robert B. Heilman's "Othello: Language and Action" in *Magic in the Web*, pp. 137–68.

12 The child psychology that follows reflects the views of the French psychoanalyst-linguist Luce Irigaray, who has proposed a theory of how the child passes from a specular to a linguistic sense of self by acquiring a mastery of first names, then shifters. See Jean-Jacques Lecercle's account of her theory in *Philosophy Through the Looking-Glass* (La Salle, Ill.: Open Court, 1985), pp. 59–61, and the Irigaray article on which his account is based, "Communication linguistique et communication spéculaire," in *Cahiers pour l'Analyse* (Paris) 3 (1966).

13 Or, rather, that is what my first or personal name does; when a child acquires a family name, becoming not merely a "John" or "Jane" but a member of the class "Doe," he or she acquires a social dimension that will prepare the way for his or her understanding of shifters.

14 On shifters, see E. Benveniste's article in his *Problems in General Linguistics*, trans. M. E. Meek (Coral Gables: University of Miami Press, 1971) and Roman Jacobson, "Shifters, Verbal Categories and the Russian Verb," in *Selected Writings II* (The Hague, 1971), pp. 130–47. See also Umberto Eco's discussion of mirrors in light of Lacan in his *Semiotics and the Philosophy of Language* (London: Macmillan, 1984), pp. 202–26.

15 The one occasion is a public one, when Othello says in a rather dampening businesslike manner, "I have but an hour / Of love, of worldly matters and direction, / To spend with thee" (1.3.301). Of course Shakespeare cannot write an entire play without allowing Desdemona some access to the *I*, but it is a suggestive way to introduce the lovers.

16 The most notable studies in the demystification of sight as against the other senses are by Walter J. Ong, S. J.; see his *Ramus: Method and the Decay of Dialogue* (Cambridge: Harvard University Press, 1958), esp. pp. 307–18; *The Presence of the Word* (New Haven and London: Yale University Press, 1967), esp. pp. 111–75; and *Interfaces of the Word* (Ithaca and London: Cornell University Press, 1977), esp. " 'I See What You Say': Sense Analogues for Intellect," pp. 121–44. See also Marshall McLuhan, *The Gutenberg Galaxy* (Toronto: University of Toronto Press, 1962), and Eric A. Havelock, *Preface to Plato* (Cambridge: Belknap Press, 1963), esp. pp. 197–233. I am particularly indebted to Ong in the following discussion of the relation of sight to sound.

17 This gives another slant on the "death of the author" brought about by writing. It is not merely that the author is absent-dead and has no authority but that he or she has been reduced from a living, speaking voice to a series of visual marks on a page, just as words reduce their referents from cats and dogs and pipes and sealing wax to verbal symbols (the point is made

visually by René Magritte's painting of a pipe across which is written the words "Ceci n'est pas une pipe.")

18   The "pen/penis" metaphor is mentioned by Eric Partridge in *Shakespeare's Bawdy* (New York: E. P. Dutton and Co., 1960), who cites *Merchant*, 5.1.237, "I'll mar the young clerk's pen." See also *All's Well*, 2.1.77, and Sonnet 16, line 10, and Sonnet 78, line 3.

19   In "Painting Women: Images of Femininity in Jacobean Tragedy," *Theatre Journal* 36, no. 3 (October 1984), Laurie A. Finke argues persuasively that Renaissance poets and playwrights often aestheticized women to death. That is, by romanticizing women as objects of eternal beauty—paintings, statues, and the like—poets immortalized them in art while killing them off as human beings.

20   To be accurate, Bacon did not entirely equate seeing with believing. He regarded sensory evidence, especially visual evidence, as crucial, but only as a recorder of experimental results. More conscious than Othello of the waywardness of the senses, he left the final judgment to reason: "But all the truer kind of interpretation of nature is effected by instances and experiments fit and apposite: wherein the sense decides touching the experiment only, and the experiment touching the point in nature and the thing itself" (*Novum Organum*, Bk. 1, Aph. 50, in *Works*, ed. John MacKinnon Robertson, p. 267)—cited by Ernst Cassirer in *The Platonic Renaissance in England*, trans. James P. Pettegrove (Austin: University of Texas Press, 1953), p. 47.

21   Desdemona's case reflects the general plight of Jacobean women in respect of speech. As Peter Stallybrass quotes from Toste's "marginal gloss to his translation of Varchi's *The Blazon of Jealousie*" ("Patriarchal Territories," p. 126):

> Maides must be seene, not heard, or selde or never,
> O may I such one wed, if I wed ever.
> A Maide that hath a lewd Tongue in her head,
> Worse than if she were found with a Man in bed.

Or as Catherine Belsey somewhat spatially puts it (*The Subject of Tragedy* [London and New York: Methuen, 1985], p. 149):

> Able to speak, to take up a subject-position in discourse, . . . [women] were nonetheless enjoined to silence, discouraged from any form of speech which was not an act of submission to the authority of their fathers or husbands. Permitted to break their silence in order to acquiesce in the utterances of others, women were denied any single place from which to speak for themselves.

22   *Ben Jonson*, ed. C. H. Herford, Percy Simpson, and Evelyn Simpson (Oxford: Clarendon Press, 1947), 8: 620–21. Jane Donaworth discusses Elizabethan attitudes toward language in Chapter 3 of her *Shakespeare and the Sixteenth-Century Study of Language* (Urbana and Chicago: University of Illinois Press, 1984), pp. 106–40; and Philip C. McGuire begins a book

about silences by emphasizing the distinctiveness of speech as a sign of life
(*Speechless Dialect: Shakespeare's Open Silences* [Berkeley and Los Angeles:
University of California Press, 1985), pp. xiii–xiv.

23 See Heilman, *Magic in the Web*, pp. 108 ff. for an extended
analysis of the obliteration of Othello's manhood.

IV. Signs, Speech, and Self

1 Baldesar Castiglione, *The Book of the Courtier*, trans. Charles S.
Singleton (Garden City, N.Y.: Anchor Books, 1959), pp. 336–48, esp.
pp. 342–47. Bembo acknowledges that there are cases in which the beautiful
are also wicked but holds that in such cases wickedness has perverted the
natural goodness of beauty.

2 Ibid., pp. 338–39.

3 Henry J. Webb, *Elizabethan Military Science: The Books and
Practice* (Madison, Milwaukee, and London: University of Wisconsin Press,
1965), p. 84.

4 Mark Rose brings this point to my attention in private correspondence, adding, "Nancy Vickers mentioned the role of the ensign as a
flag-bearer in a paper at the Shakespeare Association meeting last year [1986],
but whether she made the more general point about sign and identity I don't
recall." Professor Vickers's paper is as yet unpublished, as far as I can tell.

5 Michael Neill emphasizes the French meaning of *lieutenant* and
the various ways in which Cassio qualifies for the title, most notably of course
because he is presumed to act in lieu of Othello with Desdemona—see his
"Changing Places in *Othello*," pp. 120–21.

6 If there is anything barbaric about the Moor, it is not his language. (The word *barbarian*, as Herodotus says, derives from the fact that to
the Greeks the speech of outsiders sounded like *bar-bar-bar*.) For analyses
stressing language in *Othello* see Matthew N. Proser, *The Heroic Image in Five
Shakespearean Tragedies* (Princeton: Princeton University Press, 1965), pp.
92–135; Terence Hawkes, *Shakespeare's Talking Animals* (London: Edward
Arnold, 1973), pp. 132–42; Lawrence Danson, *Tragic Alphabet* (New Haven:
Yale University Press, 1974), pp. 97–121; Madelon Gohlke, "'All that is
spoke is marred': Language and Consciousness in *Othello*," *Women's Studies*
9 (1982): 157–76; and Harold E. Toliver's chapter on the play in his forthcoming *Transported Language in Shakespeare and Milton* (University Park and
London: Pennsylvania State University Press, 1988).

7 "The Othello Music" is the title of G. Wilson Knight's chapter
on the play in his *The Wheel of Fire* (1930; New York: Meridian Books, 1957).
Of course Iago puts a different light on Othello's rhetoric when he speaks of it
as "bombast circumstance / Horribly stuffed with epithets of war" (1.1.14).

8 All of Shakespeare's presumably crude speakers speak well in
the cause of inarticulacy. Still, Othello contrasts with, say, Coriolanus, who

not only proclaims his indifference to fine words but also truculently avoids occasions where they are to be used either about him or by him. Othello has a naive trust in the honesty of words that Coriolanus would scorn. Terence Hawkes makes a useful distinction between the plain spoken "language of men" which characterizes Othello early in the play and the duplicitous language of "manliness" which he is taught by Iago (*Shakespeare's Talking Animals*, pp. 132–42).

9   Oliver Sacks, *The Man Who Mistook His Wife for a Hat* (New York: Harper and Row, 1987), p. 111. See also in this respect Stephen J. Greenblatt's article on narrative self-fashioning in *Othello:* "Improvisation and Power" in *Literature and Society*, ed. Edward W. Said (Baltimore and London: Johns Hopkins University Press, 1980), pp. 57–99, esp. p. 73.

10   Kenneth Burke, *A Grammar of Motives and A Rhetoric of Motives* (Cleveland and New York: World Publishing Company, 1962), pp. 7–9.

11   For a perceptive analysis of *Othello* based on the rhetorical and juridical implications of "dilation" and "delation," in which the meanings of accusation, amplification, and delay combine, see Patricia Parker's "Shakespeare and Rhetoric: 'dilation' and 'delation' in *Othello*," in Parker and Hartman, *Shakespeare and the Question of Theory*, pp. 54–74.

12   This is a point of some relevance to Shakespeare as well. Who could be more conscious than he of the fact that the words you command define your identity? Out of his poetic words materialized not only theatrical performances but such self-defining properties as New Place, the cottage on the south side of Chapel Lane, 107 acres of arable land in Old Stratford, a lucrative lease of tithes of corn, grain, and hay, and of course a coat of arms and rights to the title of "Master."

13   Calling these two subjects the "speaking" and the "grammatical" is a desperate attempt to evade "the subject of the enunciation" and "the subject of the enunciating," as they are called in linguistics.

14   This view of the self as composing speech and being composed by it strikes a balance between the contemporary arguments about our using or being used by language and by other impersonal systems operating on and through us. Marxist critics in particular—reacting to their suspicion that the concept of capitalistic private ownership underlies the extreme romantic and bourgeois individualism that extols "originality" and the authority of the author—have so stressed intertextuality, contextuality, and the "production" of texts that writing is in danger of becoming not only an intransitive activity but an inhuman one as well. It goes without saying that language speaks through authors (and through plowmen and auto mechanics) and that authors can be regarded as points of convergence for diverse ideological, social, and economic formations. But although language ought to have, it did not speak with the same vocabulary, style, and eloquence through Barnaby Googe as it did through Shakespeare; and the ideological, social, and economical forces in Stratford that converged on Gilbert as well as on William

Shakespeare perhaps ought to have but did not produce a jointly written *Hamlet* and *King Lear*.

15 For the full range of the meanings of *honest* in *Othello*, see William Empson's chapter in his *The Structure of Complex Words* (Norfolk, Conn., 1951).

16 Mark Rose discusses *Othello* as a recapitulation and subversion of Shakespeare's earlier representations of chivalry in the history plays (and of Elizabethan England's efforts to "turn reality into a romance"); see "Othello's Occupation," pp. 293–311.

17 Peter Stallybrass makes an excellent case for the metaphoric significance of these particular bodily parts in terms of "the body geography of the Renaissance" in his "Patriarchal Territories," pp. 138–39.

18 The nearest analog to this moment in *Othello* is Lear's howling entrance with Cordelia's dead body, which can be regarded as part of a pattern of linguistic uncreation (as I have done in "Creative Uncreation in *King Lear*," *Shakespeare Quarterly* 37, no. 1 [Spring 1986]: 616–36).

19 Luther's scatological notions of the Devil are discussed by Norman O. Brown, *Life Against Death*, pp. 177–304.

20 Robert K. Logan, *The Alphabetic Effect* (New York: William Morrow and Co., 1986), p. 217.

21 McLuhan, *The Gutenberg Galaxy* (Toronto: University of Toronto Press, 1962), p. 164.

22 In this respect Othello more resembles Gloucester than Lear—the blind Gloucester deceived by Edgar at Dover "Cliffs," although he is cast into furious despair, not rescued from it.

23 See Mikhail Bakhtin, especially *Speech Genres and Other Essays*, trans. Vern McGee (Austin: University of Texas Press, 1986), and *Bakhtin: Essays and Dialogues on His Work*, ed. Gary Saul Morson (Chicago and London: University of Chicago Press, 1986). Actually in Bakhtin's view there is no such thing as monologue, since all utterance answers and is answerable, but I use the term for convenience.

24 As Bakhtin says, arguing against Saussure's *langue:* "Can the expressive aspect of speech be regarded as a phenomenon of *language* as a system? Can one speak of the expressive aspect of language units, i.e., words and sentences? The answer to these questions must be a categorical 'no.' . . . The word *darling*—which is affectionate both in the meaning of its root and its suffix—is in itself, as a language unit, just as neutral as the word *distance*" (*Speech Genres and Other Essays*, pp. 60; excerpted in *Bakhtin: Essays and Dialogues on His Work*, p. 96). More succinctly: "If an individual word is pronounced with expressive intonation it is no longer a word, but a complete utterance expressed by one word" (p. 62). In other words, I take it, you can define a word in a dictionary and indicate its grammatical functions, but you cannot assign it a suprasegmental phoneme that represents its prosodic meaning—you cannot say how it is to be uttered. Only on a given occasion,

spoken with a certain duration, pitch, and intensity, will *darling* escape its lexical abstractness and express affection, contempt, surprise, passion, or the emptiness of the formulaic Hollywood greeting.

V. Othello's Occupation

1   See Eric Partridge's comments on *occupation* and *occupy* in *Shakespeare's Bawdy*, p. 160. In Neill's "Changing Places in *Othello*," the pun on *occupation* is writ large.

2   On the one hand, A. C. Bradley, *Shakespearean Tragedy* (London: Macmillan and Co., 1904); Helen Gardner, "The Noble Moor," *Proceedings of the British Academy* 41 (1955); John Bayley, *The Characters of Love* (New York: Basic Books, 1960) and *The Uses of Division* (London: Chatto and Windus, 1976); John Holloway, *The Story of the Night* (Lincoln: University of Nebraska Press, 1961); and Reuben Brower, *Hero and Saint: Shakespeare and the Graeco-Roman Heroic Tradition* (New York: Oxford University Press, 1971). And on the other, T. S. Eliot, "Shakespeare and the Stoicism of Seneca" (1927), in *Selected Essays of T. S. Eliot* (New York: Harcourt, Brace & World, Inc. and Faber and Faber Ltd., 1932); Allardyce Nicoll, *Studies in Shakespeare* (London: Hogarth Press, 1931); F. R. Leavis, "Diabolic Intellect and the Noble Hero: or The Sentimentalist's Othello," *Scrutiny* 6 (1937): 259–83; Kirschbaum, "The Modern Othello"; and Heilman, *Magic in the Web*. Heilman in particular attempts to keep the balance between nobility and ignobility, as for that matter does Jane Adamson in her thoughtful study, *Othello as Tragedy: Some Problems of Judgement and Feeling* (Cambridge: Cambridge University Press, 1980).

3   As I mentioned much earlier, Shakespeare was still in an age when nobility and honor retained a close connection with *the* nobility. Surely this was true of propriety, which could be defined at first as being simply how the propertied class behaved and only later as a standard to which the propertied and unpropertied alike were constrained. Even though a barbarian of sorts, Othello fetches his life from "men of royal siege" (1.2.21). However, Roderigo and, to a lesser extent, Cassio testify to the fact that propriety and nobility do not automatically attend property and aristocracy. For instance, Cassio's foolishness about reputation takes a meaner shape in the pseudo-nobility that dismissively orders Bianca to copy the work in Othello's handkerchief and bursts out in locker room laughter at the thought that she, a "customer," might aspire to marry him.

4   It is interesting that Desdemona's image of seeing *through* Othello's black face to register a purer platonic visage in his mind implicitly acknowledges the stereotypes of blackness while claiming to transcend them. That "black is the badge of hell" (*LLL*, 4.3.350), or at least a token of evil, is accepted by everyone, even Othello.

5   For an insightful discussion of Iago as Othello's shadow, see Yasuhiro Ogawa, " 'This Forked Plague': The Meaning of Comedy in

Othello," *Essays in Foreign Languages and Literature* (Hokkaido University) (1980): 273–311.

6   This metaphor of shadowing—of *whore* as the shadow of *abhor* and of Iago as the shadow of Othello—appears elsewhere of course. Bianca is literally the whorish shadow of the abhorring Desdemona, and the drunken Cassio is the shadow of Cassio the proper man. Only Iago has no shadow; he *is* the shadow. Or perhaps we could say that the Iago of soliloquy and aside is the shadow of the honest Iago everyone else construes him to be, as well as being Othello's shadow.

7   Dusinberre, *Shakespeare and the Nature of Women*, pp. 118–20.

8   As Graham Bradshaw kindly brought to my attention. See too Alice Griffin, *The Sources of Ten Shakespearean Plays* (New York: Thomas Y. Crowell, 1966): "At this the Moor joyfully embraced her, and kissing her lovingly, exclaimed: 'God keep you long in such love, dearest wife!' In a short while, having made all necessary preparations, he set sail with his wife and troops, and after a smooth crossing arrived in Cyprus" (p. 229).

9   Edward A. Snow, "Sexual Anxiety and the Male Order of Things in *Othello,*" *English Literary Renaissance* 10 (1980):388. Snow makes an impressive case for the repression of not merely female but of male sexuality also as a cause of Othello's tragedy. Stephen J. Greenblatt stresses the fact that sexuality is conventionally regarded as shameful even within marriage—in his *Renaissance Self-Fashioning*, pp. 232–54. And Stanley Cavell argues that Othello "is horrified by sexuality, in himself and in others" because it implies his own imperfect finitude and dependence (*Disowning Knowledge in Six Plays of Shakespeare* [Cambridge: Cambridge University Press, 1987], p. 137).

10   As Heilman says, Othello ignores all the sordid gory facts of battle in favor of "visual and auditory glamor—a parade-ground war" (*Magic in the Web*, pp. 186–87). Or, in the emphasis I am putting on it, he views war as a transcendence of its most essential aspect, death.

11   Canetti, *Crowds and Power*, p. 227.

12   For detailed arguments against the consummation of the marriage, see William Whallon, *Inconsistencies* (Cambridge and Totowa, N.J.: D. S. Brewer and Biblio, 1983), pp. 68–81, and T. G. A. Nelson and Charles Haines, "Othello's Unconsummated Marriage," *Essays in Criticism* 33 (January 1983): 1–18.

13   The fact that even Cassio turns pugnacious when drunk suggests that violence is not peculiar to the Moor but to men in general. The only person in whom sexual frustration might conceivably be said to generate violence is Roderigo.

14   Plato, *The Republic* 9.571, in *Plato: The Collected Dialogues*, ed. Edith Hamilton and Huntington Cairns (Princeton: Princeton University Press, 1963), p. 798.

15   Snow, "Sexual Anxiety and the Male Order of Things in *Othello*," p. 410. The quote within the quote is from K. W. Evans, "The Racial Factor in *Othello*," *Shakespeare Survey* 5 (1965): 139.

16   Heilman has some typically perceptive remarks about the sexual aspects of the murder scene in *Magic in the Web*, pp. 187–93.

17   Blaise Pascal, *Pensées*, no. 144.

VI. Iterance

1   Mary Douglas, *Purity and Danger*, cited in Gilman, *Difference and Pathology*, p. 19.

2   In "Sexual Anxiety and the Male Order of Things in *Othello*," Snow argues that "Iago's plan is to get Othello to imagine Cassio in his (Othello's) place. What makes the strategy so effective is the way it brings Othello to see *himself* in this fantasized Cassio" (p. 394).

3   For an extended account of Iago as lover, see Heilman, *Magic in the Web*, pp. 176–79, 200–208. Neill has a fine interpretation of Iago's wooing of Othello as an aspect of a general pattern of, as his title puts it, "Changing Places in *Othello*."

4   Susan Letzler Cole, *The Absent One: Mourning Ritual, Tragedy, and the Performance of Ambivalence* (University Park and London: Pennsylvania State University Press, 1985), p. 152.

5   Howard Felperin treats this role-playing very perceptively as a matter of allegorization and deallegorization in his *Shakespearean Representation* (Princeton: Princeton University Press, 1977), pp. 74–86. See also Heilman, *Magic in the Web*, for an analysis of Othello's role-playing from the Murder Scene on.

6   Alexander Nehamas, *Nietzsche: Life as Literature* (Cambridge and London: Harvard University Press, 1985), p. 180.

7   See Daniel Keyes, *The Minds of Billy Milligan* (New York: Random House, 1981).

8   The notion that Othello is owned by what he owns (Desdemona) contributes to the dissolution of the self. The question is "At what point do our possessions end and our selves begin?" As with the concept of emotions or diseases and their symptoms, the self seems to disappear into its possessions when we define property as not merely horses and houses but spouses, jobs, bodies, feelings, and even personalities and identities, all of which we "have" or possess.

9   Neill, "Changing Places in *Othello*," p. 127.

10   In "Psychoanalysis and Renaissance Culture," in *Literary Theory and Renaissance Texts*, ed. Patricia Parker and David Quint (Baltimore: Johns Hopkins University Press, 1986), Stephen J. Greenblatt cites a surprising anticipation of this view in Thomas Hobbes's emphasis on the self as social persona: "But for Hobbes there is no person, no coherent, enduring

identity, beneath the mask; strip away the theatrical role and you reach either a chaos of unformed desire that must be tamed to ensure survival or a dangerous assembly of free thoughts . . . that must—again to ensure survival—remain unspoken" (p. 222). Greenblatt has himself done a great deal, especially in *Renaissance Self-Fashioning*, to replace naive notions about the autonomous self with a quasi-Lacanian view of the self as a product of discourse. See also Louis Montrose, "The Elizabethan Subject and the Spenserian Text," in Parker and Quint, *Literary Theory and Renaissance Texts*, and Belsey, *The Subject of Tragedy*, pp. 93–128.

11   For ritual returns see Mircea Eliade, *Le Mythe de l'éternel retour: archétypes et répétition* (Paris: Librairie Gallimard, 1949); English version, *Cosmos and History: The Myth of the Eternal Return* (New York: Harper and Brothers, 1959); see also his *Myth and Reality*, trans. Willard R. Trask (New York: Harper and Row, 1963), esp. pp. 75–91.

12   Sigmund Freud, *Beyond the Pleasure Principle*, trans. James Strachey (New York: W. W. Norton, 1961), p. 32.

13   Hunter, "Elizabethans and Foreigners," p. 51.

14   On the other hand, Hunter says "With poetic justice, the Christian reality reasserts its superior position over the pagan appearance, not in terms that can be lived through, but at least in terms that can be understood" ("Othello and Colour Prejudice," p. 161).

VII. The Properties of the Play

1   Stanley Edgar Hyman sums up the critical line from Hazlitt through Hudson, Bradley, and Granville-Barker to Kenneth Burke in his chapter "Iago and Prospero," in *Iago: Some Approaches to the Illusion of His Motivation* (London: Elek Books Ltd, 1971). On Iago's artistry, see William Hazlitt, *Characters of Shakespeare's Plays* (Boston: Wells and Lilly, 1818), pp. 60–76; A. C. Bradley, *Shakespearean Tragedy*, 2d ed. (1904: reprint ed., London: Macmillan, 1908), pp. 175–242; Harley Granville-Barker, *Prefaces to Shakespeare*, 2 vols. (Princeton: Princeton University Press, 1947), vol. 2, esp. pp. 98–112; Harold Goddard, *The Meaning of Shakespeare*, 2 vols. (Chicago: Chicago University Press, 1951), 2: 69–106; Heilman, *Magic in the Web*, esp. "The Iago World: Styles in Deception," pp. 45–98; and Sidney Homan, *When the Theater Turns to Itself* (East Brunswick, N.J.: Associated University Presses, 1981), pp. 104–20, and his "Coda on *A Midsummer Night's Dream* and *Othello*," in *Shakespeare's Theater of Presence* (Lewisburg, Pa.: Bucknell University Press, 1986), pp. 196–202.

2   Hyman, *Iago*, p. 61.

3   Janette Dillon makes the insightful observation about Richard III that his breaking free from the illusion of reality during his soliloquies parallels his breaking free from the social and moral order in England; see her

chapter on *Richard III* in *Shakespeare and the Solitary Man* (Totowa, N.J.: Rowman and Littlefield, 1981), pp. 49–60, esp. p. 59.

4   Speaking of Iago's *non serviam* stresses of course his diabolic rebellion, not against God but against standards of morality and decency usually held to take their source in divinity. Similarly, Othello the Christian convert does not lose his faith in God but in an earthly substitute, the "divine Desdemona." See in this connection Norman Rabkin, *Shakespeare and the Common Understanding,* pp. 57–73.

5   Bert O. States, *Great Reckonings in Little Rooms: On the Phenomenology of Theater* (Berkeley and Los Angeles: University of California Press, 1985), p. 125. See also the chapter "The World on Stage" for a brilliant discussion of signs and images in the theater.

6   David M. Zesmer, *Guide to Shakespeare* (New York: Barnes and Noble, 1976), p. 309. On the other hand, H. A. Mason regards the play as badly constructed (*Shakespeare's Tragedies of Love* [London: Chatto and Windus, 1970], pp. 59–162); and Ned B. Allen argues that Shakespeare wrote the play rather backwards, the last three acts first, the first two last (which accounts, he feels, for the so-called double time scheme)—"The Two Parts of *Othello,*" *Aspects of Othello,* ed. Kenneth Muir and Philip Edwards (Cambridge: Cambridge University Press, 1977), originally published in *Shakespeare Survey* 21 (1968).

7   Robert B. Heilman and Bernard Spivack have addressed the question of Iago's motivation most thoroughly, in *Magic in the Web* (pp. 25–44), and in *Shakespeare and the Allegory of Evil* (New York and London: Columbia University Press, 1958), pp. 3–25.

8   Psychoanalytic critics in particular have not been content with Coleridge's "motiveless malignity." On the whole they locate the source of Iago's evil in sadism and homosexuality. See for instance Martin Wangh, "*Othello:* The Tragedy of Iago," *Psychoanalytic Quarterly* 19 (1950): 202–12; Shelley Orgel, "Iago," *American Imago* 25 (1968): 258–74; Robert Rogers, "Endopsychic Drama in *Othello,*" *Shakespeare Quarterly* 20 (1969): 205–16; M. D. Faber, "*Othello:* The Justice of It Pleases," *American Imago* 28 (1971): 228–46; and Leslie Y. Rabkin and Jeffrey Brown, "Some Monster in His Thought: Sadism and Tragedy in *Othello,*" *Literature and Psychology* 23 (1973): 59–67. See also Randolph Splitter, "Language, Sexual Conflict, and 'Symbiosis Anxiety' in *Othello,*" *Mosaic* 15, no. 3 (1982): 17–26.

9   Aristotle's remarks on causation take their most concentrated form in *Physics,* Book 2 and *passim; Metaphysics,* Book 5; and *Posterior Analytics,* Book 2.

10   Burke, "Psychology and Form," in *Counter-Statement* (1931; Berkeley and Los Angeles: University of California Press, 1968), pp. 29–44.

11   Arguments against the consummation of the marriage are presented by William Whallon, *Inconsistencies,* pp. 68–81, and by T. G. A.

Nelson and Charles Haines, "Othello's Unconsummated Marriage," pp. 1–18.

12   In his study of *Othello*, "The Stake of the Other," Stanley Cavell says "My guiding hypothesis about the structure of the play is that the thing *denied our sight* throughout the opening scene—the thing, the scene, that Iago takes Othello back to again and again, retouching it for Othello's enchafed imagination—is what we are shown in the final scene, the scene of the murder" (p. 132).

13   For a discussion of the prevalence and incorrectness of this communicative metaphor, see Michael Reddy, "The Conduit Metaphor," in *Metaphor and Thought*, ed. A. Ortony (Cambridge: Cambridge University Press, 1979), and George Lakoff and Mark Johnson, *Metaphors We Live By* (Chicago: University of Chicago Press, 1980), pp. 10–13.

14   Joseph Loewenstein, "The Script in the Marketplace," in *Representing the English Renaissance*, ed. Stephen J. Greenblatt (Berkeley and Los Angeles: University of California Press, 1988), p. 266. In the following discussion of ownership I'm indebted to Loewenstein's informative article. See also Gerald Eades Bentley, *The Profession of Dramatist in Shakespeare's Time, 1590–1642* (Princeton: Princeton University Press, 1971), pp. 88–110.

Index